DATE DUE

MADAM
PRESIDENT

MADAM PRESIDENT

Is America ready to send

Hillary Clinton to the White House?

SUZANNE GOLDENBERG

guardianbooks

3 1218 00417 5536

First published in 2007 by Guardian Books
119 Farringdon Road, London EC1R 3ER
guardianbooks.co.uk

Guardian Books is an imprint of Guardian News and Media Ltd.

Photo credits: Insert p. 1 main picture: Polaris; p. 1 bottom left:
Lee Balterman/Time Life Pictures/Getty Images; p. 2 top: Stewart
Mike/Corbis Sygma; p. 2 bottom: Peter Blakely/Corbis Saba; p. 3 top:
AP Photo/Doug Mills; p. 3 bottom: Scott J. Ferrell/Congressional
Quarterly/Getty Images; p. 4 top: C.J. Gunther/AFP/Getty Images;
p. 4 bottom: Chip Somodevilla/Getty Images

A catalogue record for this book is available from the British Library.

ISBN: 978-0-85265-089-9

Designed and set by seagulls.net
Printed and bound in Great Britain by MPG Books, Bodmin, Cornwall

For Tony, who was always there,
and for Petra, for the times when I wasn't there

INTRODUCTION

Imagine this: it's a crisp winter day, the morning of January 20 2009, and on the steps of the US Capitol, a woman wearing her hair in a sleek blond cut and dressed in a black trouser suit raises her right hand to swear an oath of office as president of the United States. A phalanx of police officers on motorcycles rev their engines and flash their lights and the presidential motorcade heads off down Pennsylvania Avenue towards the White House.

She's back – because of course the woman on the steps of the Capitol in this particular political fantasy is Hillary Clinton. Eight years after she left the White House as the lesser-known and less popular half of the world's most famous baby boomer couple – Bill and Hillary Clinton – this is the triumphant return. As fantasies go, however, this one does not seem that far-fetched.

Come November 2008, Americans may well find themselves voting for a woman presidential candidate.

They may even elect her. In so doing they would be fulfilling what Clinton has to some extent regarded as her destiny. In her memoir *Living History*, she offered a rare moment of introspection on her place in the universe. "I represented a fundamental change in the way women functioned in our society," she wrote.

Being America's first woman president would of course be the most fundamental change of all, for the country as well as for Clinton. What is less clear is whether Clinton has been an agent of change – as she claims – or the beneficiary of changes under way in society during her lifetime.

Clinton's professional biography is a catalogue of firsts. She came of age with mid-20th century feminism, leaving for college two years after the publication of Betty Friedan's *The Feminine Mystique*. She entered Yale law school at a time when the professional world was just beginning to include women in large numbers. She was the first wife of a southern governor to pursue a legal career of her own. She was the first First Lady to try to wield an open and direct influence over administration policy. She was the first First Lady to run for high office. As a senator, she has been part of a small group of women trying to operate in an institution that has yet to fully catch up with most workplaces in its attitude towards sexual equality.

All of these are admirable achievements. And yet there is something about Hillary Clinton that can make the most rational people become unhinged. I've lost count of the number of times while writing this book I've been asked, with suspicion, "But do you like her?" as people try to gauge whether I have set out on a hatchet job or a hagiography. Or how often I have been asked what further revelations there are to dredge from an already over-examined marriage. With Clinton, there seems to be no in-between. Some men find her threatening; for some women she is absolutely infuriating. As I was finishing this book, I went to dinner at the house of friends in Arlington, Virginia, one of the suburbs of Washington, and got into conversation with a warm and engaging civil servant and mother of two. She was a committed Democrat, one who despaired at the state of the country under George W Bush. In the small-town way of Washington, she was personally acquainted with people on Hillary Clinton's campaign. But as she began to explain, calmly at first while she rounded up her two boys for the journey home, she found she harboured a great deal of anger at the woman. She was unable to forgive her for taking Bill back after he so publicly humiliated her with his affair with the White House intern Monica Lewinsky. "She should have castrated him," the civil servant hissed.

In August 1998 I watched Monicagate unspool from Afghanistan, where Bill Clinton had ordered air strikes against suspected al-Qaida bases in retaliation for the bombings of two US embassies in East Africa. I did not see Hillary Clinton in the flesh until long after she had left the White House. She was a senator by then and speaking at a gala event at the Kennedy Centre in Washington. It was May 2003 and I had recently returned from Baghdad, where I covered the final days of Saddam Hussein's regime and the arrival of the first US marines. I was curious to see the woman people were already speaking of as presidential material – the woman who had voted for the war I had just returned from. In the cavernous gloom of the Kennedy Centre, it was difficult to see what others had: Clinton did not radiate charisma – at least not as far as the back rows where I was sitting. I cannot remember what she said. She looked entirely ordinary, mere mortal.

And yet she has come closer than any woman before her to the pinnacle of American political power. How much of that success is of Clinton's own making? How much is down to chance? And in that circuitous route to the top, what compromises was Clinton forced to make?

By the time she ran for the presidency, Clinton had accumulated another set of histories that were the antithesis of her academic and professional achievements. She had spent 25 years serving her husband's political ambitions instead of her own, and had dedicated herself to a marriage that many women saw as degrading. She had suffered a tremendous setback in her attempts to remake the role of First Lady into a career position. Yes, she had redeemed herself by being elected to the Senate, and winning over the people of New York state. But it was true also that Hillary would not have had a whisper of hope of being elected senator if she had not been married to Bill.

She was running a near-faultless campaign for president. But her greatest credential – her eight-year stay in the White House – was also a by-product of her marriage.

For Clinton, as for many women in America and the world, the path to political power has not been simple or straightforward. It's a path marked as much by circumstance as by personal character. It's by exploring the junction of the two – character and circumstance – that it is possible to really see the forces that created the woman we now know as Hillary Clinton, the candidate, and that could guide the actions of the woman we may one day know as Madam President.

PART ONE

WOMAN'S HOUR

It was about 20 minutes into the presidential debate when Hillary Clinton was asked the series of questions that made the women watching in Melody Drnach's apartment sit up a little straighter on the cream-coloured sofa, set down their wine glasses, and call for the volume on the TV set to be turned up.

The first televised debates of the 2008 election season had been polite and relatively bloodless. This bout between Democratic hopefuls on a Monday evening in July 2007 could have gone in almost any direction. The questions to the candidates came from members of the public, who had posted videos on YouTube before the debate. The results were a break from the bland caution of television professionals. Among the videos selected for broadcast, a cancer sufferer pulled a wig off her bald head, and a man from a long line of soldiers displayed the flag that had covered the coffin of his eldest son, who had been killed in Iraq.

But the women gathered in Drnach's apartment in Washington's Foggy Bottom neighbourhood were still taken aback at the line of inquiry directed at Clinton. They may have been obvious questions, but there was still something unexpected about a candidate for the US presidency being asked: Are you woman enough to be in the White House? And, if you do get elected, how can we be sure you would do a better job for women than any of the male candidates? How would you negotiate with leaders of Muslim states where women do not enjoy equal rights? Clinton didn't miss a beat. "There isn't much doubt in anyone's mind that I can be taken seriously," she said. It seemed for a moment as if the planets were re-aligning – that the qualifications for leadership were about to change.

Drnach, a vice-president at the National Organisation for Women (Now), who was wearing a Make History T-shirt from the Clinton campaign, was so excited she jumped out of her seat. "That's what having a woman in the race does. Can you imagine? I think it's terrific that they are up there arguing about who is going to be a better president for women."

The singularity of Clinton's candidacy was not always expressed in ways that Drnach would have liked. On the day of the debate, the most talked-about news story was a fashion item in the Washington Post deconstructing Clinton's neckline. Did that sliver of flesh above her V-neck top – as seen on C-Span – really constitute cleavage; and if so, what was its message? Was Clinton deliberately trying to present herself as a powerful, sexy woman? Did this signal a new self-confidence in the senator from New York? But Clinton's run for the White House was raising serious questions as well. Women cast 54 per cent of the votes in the 2004 presidential elections. A network of well-funded organisations with close ties to both main parties had been working for years to get more women into elected office. And yet, until Clinton, no woman had ever had a serious chance of being elected president. In 2007 the representation of women in the US Congress was just 16 per cent, well behind other industrialised nations. Why, in a country that prides itself on being a land of opportunity, had it taken so long for a woman to rise to Clinton's position? How would women and men respond to her candidacy? If Americans did elect their first woman president in 2008, how would Clinton be any different from the 43 men who had occupied the White House before her?

On screen, Clinton barely paused for breath. Wearing a salmon-coloured jacket that produced the one splash of colour in a row of dark suits, she talked about breaking glass ceilings, overcoming the reservations of Muslim world leaders, and setting an example of equality for a generation of girls and boys. Drnach let out a whoop and pumped her hand in the air. "You go, girl!" she said.

The small gathering that night was a campaign event, a debate-watching party meant to solidify women's support for Clinton. It may have looked like a casual get-together, but it was part of a sophisticated drive to sign up volunteers and build excitement about Clinton's candidacy. The strategy was already beginning to pay off. By mid-2007 Clinton had begun to pull away from her Democratic rivals in the opinion polls thanks to strong support from women. She had support from male voters, of course, but it was her advantage among women that was putting Clinton over the top. She performed well among young single women, and especially well among women in their 50s. She was also the favourite of those her campaign called "women with needs", women in relatively low-paying jobs and with only a secondary school education. College-educated and wealthy women, and especially those who, like Clinton, were entering their 60s, remained cool, but the campaign was confident they could be turned.

Before the debate began that night, Drnach had joined a conference call for a pep talk from the actor Mary Steenburgen, a friend from Clinton's Arkansas days. Clinton was the kind of person who always made a point of calling when she heard someone was in hospital, Steenburgen said; she was the best girlfriend anyone could ask for. *Girlfriend*? It's not generally considered a presidential attribute. But it got the seal of approval from the women at Drnach's place – mainly young, mainly single, mainly white and mainly professional. A couple had worked on Democratic campaigns. One confessed she was barely old enough to remember the Monica Lewinsky scandal less than a decade before.

What the women saw that night was a candidate not only capable of competing with men but assured enough to pounce on an early mistake, even in the traditionally male preserve of foreign policy. When her main rival for the Democratic nomination, Barack Obama, ventured that he would readily meet the leaders of America's enemies – Iran, Syria, Venezuela, Cuba and North Korea – Clinton swiftly cut him down to size, pointing out the danger of handing these regimes a propaganda coup. "Certainly, we're not going to just have our president meet with Fidel Castro and Hugo Chavez and, you know, the presidents of North Korea, Iran and Syria, until we know better what the way forward would be," she said.

Drnach and the others watching that night saw in Clinton a woman of steel and silk: a devoted mother and a lifelong advocate for children who was also tough on terror; a woman who had survived marriage to a man who had regularly cheated on her; a wise policy veteran thanks to her residency at the White House and her years in the Senate, who could be counted on to get down to work immediately after her election. They were also persuaded Clinton would bring change to their own lives, by encouraging other women to run for office, and creating momentum for social reform. "I am definitely leaning towards Hillary Clinton, and it's mostly the gender," said Jill Cartwright, a law student. "Just as a woman, I feel that a woman can represent my interests better – no matter how liberal or progressive a man is."

Clinton's appeal to women was widespread. In a series of focus groups conducted by the Centre for the Advancement of Women in Philadelphia, Memphis and Los Angeles, she consistently topped the list of women they most admired. Among Latina women in LA, she ranked ahead of Mother Teresa. African-American women in Philadelphia put her just behind Oprah Winfrey and the R&B singer Fantasia. White women in Memphis also gave high ratings to Clinton, along with Winfrey and a television evangelical.

Some of the women openly hated Clinton. "I think she's a pig. I think she's a liar. I think she's a cheater. I think she is insincere," said an African-American woman in Philadelphia. But there was respect in all three cities for her intellect, and her apparent calm when forced to deal with her husband's infidelities in the full glare of the media. "The whole world knew. And she handled it just perfect," one of the Latina women in Los Angeles said, describing Clinton as "a very smart lady".

Like Drnach's guests, these groups were motivated by the idea of any woman running, and of attaining the power whereby she could make a material difference in their lives. "Men don't see things in exactly the same way we see things," said an African-American woman in Philadelphia. Across the country in Memphis, a similar view prevailed. "As far as what a female president would do, I think no matter whether she was conservative or liberal or what, the fact that we had a woman president would start to help us," said one woman.

Some of the focus group members worried that Clinton would be undermined by male politicians and lobbyists, or be at a disadvantage dealing with world leaders. One woman in LA admitted that she felt uncomfortable with the thought of a woman in charge. But they looked to Clinton to bring in policies to encourage job flexibility so they could spend more time with their children. They thought that if Clinton were president she would press for on-site daycare and better funding for health services. They also thought a woman leader would be more compassionate, would act from the heart. That would lead to more liberal policies on abortion, and a greater commitment to using diplomacy to resolve international conflicts. Women were planners, several said: a woman president would not rush to war. "I hope that she would think twice," said one Latina woman in LA. "She would think as a mother: how would this affect my children, how would this affect my family?"

America had been shuffling through images of Hillary Clinton like tarot cards for 15 years by the time she declared her candidacy in January 2007. Career woman, doting mother, man-hating radical feminist, saviour of the world's downtrodden, backroom strategist, political helpmate and First Lady, betrayed wife and senator from New York: Clinton had either played those parts or been assigned them by her opponents. Now she was about to embark on her most ambitious transformation yet.

Perched among embroidered throw cushions and silver-framed family photographs in the sunroom of her

Georgetown mansion, Clinton announced she was running for president. But it was not just a declaration of a campaign; Clinton had constructed yet another persona. She was the first woman presidential candidate to have a powerful political machine behind her. It was an incarnation that demanded to be taken seriously. "I'm in. And I'm in to win," she said.

For the first time, a woman had a realistic chance of making it all the way to the presidency. Clinton was not a dissident, or an outsider, the lonely voice on the edges of her party. She was the ultimate Washington power player. Nobody else could claim to have had as close a view of the workings of the White House. Clinton had lived there for eight years, from January 1993 to January 2001. In those years as First Lady, she developed relationships with world leaders that no other candidate could match. And no other candidate could claim to have ready access to the contacts book of that natural-born schmoozer, Bill Clinton.

By July 2007, with six months to go until the Democratic primaries, Hillary Clinton had a double-digit lead in the opinion polls against her main rivals, Barack Obama and John Edwards. But she remained a polarising figure. She was viewed unfavourably by around 40 per cent of the population. Some of these so-called Hillary-haters were easy to account for. A committed Republican would never vote for a Democrat, and that held true even among women. Party loyalty trumped gender. (Republican women tend to be less enthused by women candidates.

A study of congressional races by the Pew Research Centre for People and the Press, an independent think tank, found that Republican women – unlike Democrats – were not inclined to support women candidates.)

The journalist and women's rights activist Gloria Steinem argued that support for Clinton broke along class lines. "They say you can tell a Hillary supporter by her shoes. If she is wearing nurse's shoes, or waitress's shoes, she supports Hillary. If she is wearing Manolo Blahniks or whatever those shoes are called, she may not," Steinem told me. "Overwhelmingly, women of colour, single women, poor women who have a better sense of their interest in issues, are for Hillary."

There were also male Democratic voters who harboured a strong dislike for Clinton, especially blue-collar workers. Independent male voters were cool as well – and there was a reason. Unlike almost all the other contenders lining up for the 2008 elections, Hillary Clinton was a known quantity. She had become familiar through two presidential campaigns and two presidencies. People had formed opinions about her, and some of those opinions were harsh. A few weeks into the campaign, the Pew Research Centre polled the public for their first impressions of the would-be presidents. The words that came to mind when people thought of Clinton were: Bill, husband, intelligence, and strength, but also phoney, sneaky, way too feminist, backstabber, and she-devil.

Some Democratic strategists were sanguine, arguing that any candidate as high-profile as Hillary Clinton was bound to accumulate high unfavourability ratings. Just give the other candidates time and their negative ratings would grow too, they said. But the question of likeability was generally acknowledged as the biggest weakness in Clinton's candidacy, infecting even committed Democrats. They might respect her experience, her obvious intelligence, and her grasp of policy detail – but *like* her? That might be too much to ask.

These reservations did not extend to the party establishment, where loyalists – to Bill and now Hillary – occupied important positions. By July 2007, the Clinton machine was whirring away. The candidate had $45m in the bank, and phone lists of potential supporters dating from her days at an all-women's college through her years as First Lady. She had a strong network of relationships from six years in the Senate, and from her fundraising for other Democratic candidates. She had a campaign staff drawn from among the party's top strategists, pollsters and policy advisers. And she had that biggest asset of all: her husband. Behind the scenes, he was now performing in the roles Hillary once filled for him, serving as strategist and fundraiser, and defending her against critics. The former president remained enormously popular, especially among the Democratic voters Hillary would first have to win over to gain the party's nomination. Most Americans thought he would be a good thing for his wife's campaign. If voters were unsure about how they felt about Hillary, they could reassure themselves with the thought they would be getting a piece of Bill too.

Even her enemies conceded Clinton was the best-prepared candidate. Barring an excruciating misstep on the campaign trail in the months ahead, the unearthing of a scandal, a terrible policy miscalculation, or an act of God, it was almost beginning to feel like a victory was inevitable. This was not an unqualified blessing, however: to some, the thought of Hillary Clinton in the White House was not so much a first for women as a second turn for the Clintons. The Bushes had formed a father-and-son act in the White House; did America now have to put up with a husband and wife? Amid a field of candidates who could also claim to be potential history-makers – Barack Obama as the first African-American and Bill Richardson as the first Latino on the Democratic side, and Mitt Romney as the first Mormon for Republicans – voters were reminded to ask again whether they would really be striking a blow for progress by backing Clinton. A video homage to George Orwell's *1984* surfaced on YouTube, showing rows of blank-faced automata listening to the droning voice of Hillary Clinton, the authoritarian Big Sister. The message was clear: a vote for Clinton was a vote for the status quo.

Unless, of course, you were a politically engaged woman in need of some encouragement. According to the Inter–Parliamentary Union, the United States ranks

67th – right between Zimbabwe and Turkmenistan – in terms of the representation of women. That translates into 16 per cent of the seats in Congress: 71 women members in the 435-seat House of Representatives, and 16 in the 100-seat Senate. Studies show that women in the US are much less likely to run for office than men. They are more likely to be carrying the burden of childcare. They are also hesitant to expose their family to the intense publicity of modern campaigning. But the biggest barrier is more fundamental: many women continue to think that politics is just not for them. They tend to underestimate their suitability as candidates, compared with men with similar qualifications. They tend to be less confident of winning, and so are less inclined to enter the race. They are also likely to be overlooked by party officials charged with recruiting candidates.

That reluctance to enter the fray holds true even for local and state office, which means that there are fewer women getting their first foot on the ladder that would eventually lead to a seat in a state assembly, the House of Representatives or the Senate. Campaign finance is also a problem, albeit no longer the biggest one. Party donors tend to back candidates who are seen as winners – which again means men. But organisations such as Emily's List, which raises funds for Democratic women who support abortion rights, have helped to narrow the gap. "Once we can get women to be candidates, money is not the biggest factor any more. There are still disparities, but I think the biggest problem is just getting women to throw their hat into the ring just now," said Shauna Lani Shames, who has worked at Now and the White House Project, which trains women for leadership.

The closest any woman before Clinton has come to supreme power in the United States was Geraldine Ferraro, who ran for vice-president alongside Walter Mondale on the Democratic ticket in 1984. It was and remains the first time Americans have had the chance to vote for a woman even as vice-president – although elections since have brought almost ritual speculations about which women might make the shortlist for the job. Two women were appointed and served as secretaries of state – Madeleine Albright and Condoleezza Rice – and many others have been elected as governors, senators, congresswomen and mayors. In January 2007 Nancy Pelosi, who raised five children before deciding to run for Congress from San Francisco, was elected as the first woman speaker of the House of Representatives. But no woman had ever been a viable candidate for president. "There is no question in my mind that gender was – and remains – a huge factor," said Carol Moseley Braun, whose own attempt to become the Democratic presidential candidate in 2004 collapsed before the first votes were cast. "My campaign was almost entirely inspired by my then 10-year-old niece, who was looking at her social studies books and saying: 'But Auntie Carol, all the presidents are boys.' The reality is that the social changes have been far slower than we expected, and because of that so have the changes in any real sense for women."

And while the Clinton campaign early on had all the assurance of a winner, others warned there was no guarantee that her time had come. Some women feared her candidacy would serve the same function as Ferraro's: merely paving the way for another run at some unspecified point in the future. "I just don't think that attitudes change that dramatically. I think she is blazing the trail for someone who some day can win," said Faye Wattleton, president of the Centre for the Advancement of Women. "These are deeply ingrained attitudes and positions about people."

Clinton entered the presidential race at a time when a new generation of women was challenging some of the assumptions that had guided feminist thought when she was coming of age. In the late 1960s and early 1970s, when Clinton was at college and trying to map out her own career as a lawyer, many feminists had argued that women and men had the same potential to succeed: all that was needed to produce true equality was to remove the obstacles to women's advancement. But maybe the glass ceiling – the invisible barrier that had prevented women from getting to the upper reaches of elite professions – was not the issue after all. Maybe what really mattered was changing the unwritten rules that governed the lives of everyone in the workforce. Both women and men suffered in a culture that demanded long hours and blinkered dedication to one's job to get ahead. The elusive search for happiness was reflected in a poll by the Pew Research Centre, in which sharing household chores ranked third among the ingredients of a successful marriage, behind faithfulness and a happy sex life.

Women had broken into areas that had once been off-limits. They had proven they could perform as CEOs and astronauts, soldiers and Supreme Court justices. But what changes had there really been in the lives of the majority of working women, while these few were forging ahead?

The way of working in America had become incompatible with family life, especially for women. Unlike other industrialised countries, the American workplace had made few accommodations for parenthood, offering only 12 weeks' maternity leave – unpaid. In Britain, employers are required by law to offer 39 weeks of leave, and workers receive statutory maternity pay. In France, the legal minimum for maternity leave is 16 weeks, also paid. Canada offers 17 weeks' maternity leave, covered by unemployment insurance. America also lags behind in terms of leave to care for other family members, which is unpaid. (The leave provisions were enacted only in 1993, long after women had moved into the workforce.)

With no national system of childcare or health insurance, the alternatives for women were stark. Devote oneself to one's career, or cast those ambitions aside to raise one's children: there seemed to be little ground in between. The anxiety about those alternatives surfaced in the popular arena as the Mummy Wars, with working mothers – and nearly 75 per cent of mothers remained in the workforce in some capacity – squaring up to those who had left their jobs to stay home with their children. "When a mother works, something is lost," wrote Caitlin Flanagan in a 2004 essay in the Atlantic magazine. "If she works, she can't have as deep and connected a relationship with her child as she would if she stayed home and raised him." What was largely overlooked by Flanagan and others, however, was that families in all of their configurations had been trapped by an economy that demanded a 24/7 work schedule but skimped on childcare. There was really no choice – or at least no good choice – for women. A raft of new studies showed that the American workplace was overtly hostile to the very notion of family. While the gap in wages between men and women had shrunk, a May 2007 study by sociologists at Cornell University found that mothers were 79 per cent less likely to be hired than non-mothers, and would be offered starting salaries that were $11,000 lower. Their commitment would continually be questioned, they would be held to a higher performance standard, and they would be granted no slack for lateness or missed days.

Every woman candidate has to negotiate that terrain of disappointment and expectation. But that process was especially fraught for Clinton because in some ways her rise was a reminder of the limitations on sexual equality at the beginning of the 21st century. How would her success improve the lives of women who did not have the advantage of her education and connections? "How do you build a women's movement that simultaneously encourages women to excel and pursue rewarding careers, and acknowledges the pain felt by families where neither the women nor the men have a good job and both have to work in ways that really interfere with their ability to construct a family life?" asked Stephanie Coontz, a historian specialising in the family. "That is the huge dilemma for the women's movement now that hasn't been answered. How do you support both? There is a huge class divide."

Clinton's determinedly centrist stance in the Senate and as a presidential candidate made her suspect among some women, particularly those on the left. The actor Susan Sarandon, a prominent supporter of liberal causes, was scathing. "Everybody is so cautious and just trying to get elected, just trying to stay in office, and I think she suffers from that. I think she's a politician like everyone else," she told the British journalist Jonathan Dimbleby in 2006. "I'd like to find somebody that really has a moral bottom line, be they man or woman."

Other critics accuse Clinton of betraying the women's movement, although she has repeatedly called herself a feminist and paid tribute to the efforts of earlier generations of women's activists. Elizabeth Edwards, the wife of her Democratic rival John Edwards, suggested Clinton had been so eager to scale the heights of power she had neglected the cause of women along the way. Like Clinton, Elizabeth Edwards had been a lawyer, and was familiar with the barriers women face in their careers. "Sometimes you feel you have to behave as a man and not talk about women's issues. I'm sympathetic – she wants to be commander-in-chief. But she's just not as vocal a woman's advocate as I want to see," she told the online magazine Salon.

For others – even fellow Democrats – Clinton's journey from helpmate to candidate was a source of disquiet. "I find it deeply annoying when people make her into some kind of feminist heroine," complained a lawyer from Cincinnati, Ohio, who like Clinton is entering her sixties. "This is a woman who is where she is because of who she married. I don't think she would ever have got there if she hadn't been married to him, and stuck with him, and that's fine. But that's not the feminist message you want your daughters to receive, is it? Isn't it a little old-fashioned? Pick a guy who can give you position and opportunity and access."

Plus, the lawyer said, she simply did not trust Clinton. "I think she would literally do and say anything to get and keep power, just the way she dances around on a lot of issues as if she is constantly consulting her pollsters."

The novelist Mary Gordon came up with an original explanation for why some women found the Clinton marriage so troubling. "I think no woman is electable in

America, and particularly not Hillary, because she is married to this guy whom everyone is libidinally attached to. I think there is unconscious sexual jealousy of her among women," she told the New York Times. Didn't it matter that Bill Clinton was flagrantly unfaithful, the interviewer asked. "No," Gordon replied, "because she got him in the first place."

The Christian right and anti-feminists, meanwhile, saw in Hillary Clinton a symbol of all the negative changes America had undergone over the past 40 years, and the remaking of the roles of wife and mother, husband and father. That Clinton not only survived the White House years – when both she and her husband were under regular assault from religious demagogues and rightwing talk show hosts – but actually prospered was absolutely galling. When Clinton was endorsed by Now and reclaimed her feminist credentials, a Christian women's group known as the Concerned Women of America put out a sour statement asserting: "Hillary needs a reality check if she thinks that a majority of women voters embrace radical feminism."

It would be impossible for any candidate to satisfy all of those constituencies, Marie Wilson, the director of the White House Project, told me. Wilson argues that the intense and competing views of Clinton have less to do with her personality and policies than with women wielding power. Americans continue to associate femininity with subservience, she claimed. It's what you call a double bind: if a woman leader wants to persuade voters of her grasp of "masculine" areas such as defence, she immediately risks jeopardising her reputation for being nice. "We are still fighting against things that are deep in the culture, and she is the place where we have that conversation," said Wilson. "We don't say we are concerned about ambitious women; we talk about Hillary Clinton. Because she is the first she has tested many of the issues that are really not about her, but about the deeply cultural issues that have kept women out of leadership."

For Clinton, as for any woman candidate, the challenge was to try to respond to some of those anxieties without appearing weak. But calibrating that response had become immeasurably more difficult. At a time of war, following the September 11 2001 terror attacks and the US invasions of Afghanistan and Iraq, Clinton had felt under immense pressure to convey an impression of strength and experience, and she devoted a great deal of effort to burnishing her defence credentials. Her campaign website had a section entitled Champion for Women, but as Clinton said in one of her very first web chats: "I am not looking for people to say, 'I'm going to vote for her' just because I'm a woman."

Yet it's worth considering again: until Clinton, America had still not had a serious female contender for president. That's nearly half a century after Sri Lanka delivered the world's first woman prime minister in Sirimavo Bandaranaike in 1960. Since then, 41 other countries have gone on to elect women as prime ministers and presidents. India had Indira Gandhi, and Israel Golda Meir. Britain elected Margaret Thatcher in 1979. Pakistan became the first Muslim nation to vote a woman into national office when Benazir Bhutto became prime minister in 1988. The Philippines and Bangladesh have each had two woman leaders, while back in Sri Lanka Bandaranaike's daughter, Chandrika Kumaratunge, was elected the island's first woman president in 1994. Chile, once the land of men in uniform like Augusto Pinochet, has Michelle Bachelet. Liberia has Ellen Johnson-Sirleaf. Germany has Angela Merkel, France had Edith Cresson and at least considered Ségolène Royal. North of the 49th Parallel, Canada briefly had Kim Campbell.

Some of these women owed their elevation to powerful fathers – like Gandhi, whose father, Jawaharlal Nehru, led India to independence, and Indonesia's Megawati Sukarnoputri. Others came to power as mourners following assassinations or coups – like Bandaranaike, whose husband, Solomon, was killed by a Buddhist monk in 1959. But while it's easy to mock the tendency towards dynastic power in Asia, family ties remained the most important route to the Senate for American women until the beginning of the 1990s. Until that point most women senators had acquired their seats through inheritance, appointed to replace fathers or husbands who had died in office. Even today, more than a quarter of all members of Congress have family connections in politics as the wives, widows, sisters and daughters of politicians.

So why has no American woman ever been a genuine contender for the presidency? It's not because of any lack of interested candidates. The first woman to seek the US presidency was Victoria Woodhull in 1872, nearly half a century before universal suffrage for woman in 1920. Woodhull, a stockbroker and newspaper publisher, was a candidate of the Equal Rights Party. She chose an African-American man as her running mate, the abolitionist Frederick Douglass, who was born a slave. He never accepted the offer, however, and campaigned for the re-election of Ulysses S Grant. The first woman from a main-stream party to seek the presidency was Margaret Chase Smith, a Republican from Maine who spent more than 20 years as a senator, and was an early and forceful opponent of McCarthyism. She sought the nomination in 1964, but came a distant fifth to the conservative Barry Goldwater.

Eight years later, Shirley Chisholm, the first African-American woman to be elected to the House of Representatives, ran for the Democratic nomination. She failed to win the endorsement of the black members of Congress, and struggled to raise funds to campaign. But she managed to get on the ballot in 12 states, and stay in the contest long enough to pick up a handful of votes at the Democratic convention in Miami that year. None of the women who ran for president after Chisholm made it that far. Pat Schroeder, a left-leaning member of House of Representatives from Colorado, had a brief run for the presidency in 1987, but with seven Democrats already in the race soon concluded that she could never raise enough funds to close the gap. She wept when she announced she had to pull out of the race – a display of emotion for which she is still called to account.

The 2000 elections produced a different model of woman candidate in Elizabeth Dole. A Republican, Dole seemed at the start of her campaign to be a Washington insider. She had held cabinet posts in two Republican administrations, under Ronald Reagan and the first President Bush, and further polished her résumé by spending a decade as president of the American Red Cross. She was married to a senator and one-time presidential contender, Robert Dole. But those credentials did not seem to matter once she started campaigning. "Though roughly as fragile as Margaret Thatcher, she is also famously thin-skinned, and has been known to burst into tears over unflattering press," wrote the New York Times in a piece cited in a study by the White House Project. The Times' story on George W Bush's announcement speech focused on his positions on Kosovo and tax cuts. Dole withdrew from the race months before any votes were cast when her campaign ran out of money. Although Bush reputedly put her on the shortlist of vice-presidential candidates, she was eventually passed over in favour of Dick Cheney.

Carol Moseley Braun was definitely an outsider when she entered the Democratic race in 2004. The only African-American woman ever to be elected to the Senate in 1992, she had seen her early promise eclipsed by allegations that she had missspent nearly $250,000 in campaign donations, and accusations of sexual harassment against her campaign manager, who was also her fiance. The allegations from Moseley Braun's campaign treasurer, which centred on a month-long trip to South Africa she took with her then fiance, Kgosie Matthews, and purchases of jewellery, two Jeeps, and stereo equipment, led America's tax authorities, the Internal Revenue Service, to request an investigation. The justice department blocked the inquiry. In 1997, an audit by the Federal Elections Commission faulted the campaign for sloppy financial management and compelled Ms Moseley Braun to return some contributions, but found "no material non-compliance". Moseley Braun repeatedly denied misusing campaign funds. But the controversy over campaign finance and criticism by human rights activists of a 1996 trip to Nigeria to meet the dictator, General Sani Abacha, raised doubts about her judgment.

Moseley Braun lost her Senate seat in 1998, and became ambassador to New Zealand. A late entrant into the race, Moseley Braun told me she struggled to raise funds and to be taken seriously as a candidate. Moseley Braun was quietly told that it was too risky to back a candidate who was both African-American and a woman. "There were high-profile women who said: 'Yes, we want a woman, but not just any woman.' In other words, 'Don't be silly. A candidate who is black and female? Come on!'"

She was forced to fold days before the first votes were cast when her finance manager warned her she might not be able to cover the campaign payroll.

Did Moseley Braun and the other women fail because the public won't elect a woman? Opinion polls suggest more than 90 per cent of Americans would be ready to vote for a woman president. More than half believe that America would be better off if it were led by a woman. But ask the same person if they think the *average American* is prepared to accept a woman as president, and the answer becomes rather different. Only 55 per cent of those polled said the country was ready, and among women the figure was just 51 per cent.

The different figures are reminiscent of polling on African-American candidates, where there is often a wide gap between the number who say they would vote for a black person, and those who say their friends and relatives would not. What it suggests is that there are plenty of reasons that the country is not ready to vote for a woman – even if people are not prepared to say them out loud.

Some of those obstacles come early in a politician's career – the difficult process of raising funds and getting into the race. Clinton has cleared those barriers. But other traps lie ahead. She will need to persuade Americans of both her ordinariness and her toughness if she is to avoid the fate of Geraldine Ferraro: a woman who showed the way. Here are some of the questions she still has to answer.

COULD YOU LEAD US INTO BATTLE?

Soon after Ferraro began her run for the vice-presidency, a columnist in the Denver Post called Woodrow Paige raised the horrifying prospect of what might happen should she somehow become president. "What if she is supposed to push the button to fire the missiles and she can't because she has just done her nails?" For all the buffoonery, Paige was highlighting a wider concern: the biggest stretch for most voters is imagining the idea of a woman as a warrior. The occupant of the White House is not only president of the United States, but the leader of the free world, the commander-in-chief of the last remaining superpower. For women candidates, that requires a disconnection from the traditional role of women as carers. Voters have to ask themselves if they can trust a woman to call in air strikes against al-Qaida training camps or nuclear installations in "rogue states".

National security is seen as beyond a woman's expertise. Those considerations weighed heavily on Ferraro's mind. "I couldn't make mistakes. I couldn't cry. The guys could cry. I get a kick out of the guys crying. But I had to be very careful," she told me. "We were in a cold war with the Soviet Union. I had to make sure that I was not perceived as being weak. I had to make sure that I was perceived as being smart."

The stereotypes were just as confining for women who did have a demonstrated expertise. Although

Schroeder had spent several years on the House Armed Services Committee, she was forever having to prove her military credentials. "People were still worried about defence. They said: 'You never served in the military,' and I wanted to say: 'I don't think anyone else running has either.' But somehow if you are a male it didn't matter. The commander-in-chief thing was really tough." Bill Clinton's appointment of Madeleine Albright as the first woman secretary of state, and George W Bush's appointment of Condoleezza Rice as the first African-American in the same position have worn down resistance to the idea of women conducting diplomacy. But handing a woman command of the military is another matter. In the aftermath of 9/11, the White House Project advised women candidates to tone down their caring, compassionate side, and play to images of strength.

WHY HAVEN'T WE SEEN YOU
AT THE MOVIES?

Nearly every leading man in Hollywood gets a chance to play a president. But cinematic representations of a woman in the West Wing are exceedingly rare and seldom heroic. In the totally unreconstructed 1964 film Kisses for My President, the improbably elected female leader of the free world resigns when she falls pregnant. (Her disgruntled husband, played by Fred MacMurray, rejoices that while it took the votes of millions of women to put the president in office, it took only one man to get her out.) Television recently proved more PC with Commander-in-Chief, although the show went off the air after just one season. But even Commander-in-Chief couldn't quite stretch to showing a woman beating the male competition in a presidential election. The main character, Mackenzie Allen, is a vice-president who takes over from her boss after he dies in office. She does so only after ignoring demands from political opponents and members of her own party that she step aside for someone more appropriate, ie a man. In 2007 the popular show 24 announced that its seventh season would feature a female president, but in general the closest women on screen get to the Oval Office is the vice-presidency. In the 1997 thriller Air Force One, Glenn Close plays a vice-president negotiating with hijackers holding the male president hostage – 13 years after Ferraro's run on the Democratic ticket.

CAN YOU TAKE THE PRESSURE?

No woman runs for office alone. She carries the dreams and fears of millions of others, and the response is sharp if she disappoints. When Schroeder ended her presidential campaign, she was scolded for destroying the dreams of generations of women. Women journalists said her tears had set the movement back a hundred years. Schroeder was shocked by their anger. She said: "To see that coming from young women made it clear how intensely their identification is wrapped around what you are doing. You can never be perfect enough, and the sadness was that they really believed that the only way women were going to get ahead was if they were absolutely perfect. If anyone went out and wasn't absolutely perfect, then nobody else would ever get a shot at it."

Clinton knew how harsh the media could be from her years as First Lady. At that time, the Clintons' daughter, Chelsea, was still a child, and her parents were able to declare her off-limits to the press. That truce was unlikely to hold for Clinton's own presidential run, when her daughter was in her mid-20s and working at a hedge fund in Manhattan. As any woman running for office knows, it is open season for the media on her husband, her children, and – ludicrous though it might seem – her hair and her clothes. As Barbara Mikulski, a senator from Maryland, lamented in a 1994 speech at the University of Pennsylvania: "It is always, 'Short, stocky Barbara Mikulski said aggressively …' They never say, 'The handsome, nevertheless ageing Harry Hughes, showing a trifle pot belly from sitting eight years in the state house …'" The senator went on: "Often our style is criticised. We are either too soft-spoken or too outspoken. Our marital status always becomes a subject that is negative. If you're married, the press says you're neglecting him. If you're widowed, deep down inside you really killed him. If you are divorced, you couldn't keep him, and if you are single, you couldn't get somebody in the first place."

That kind of preoccupation with women leaders is not exclusively American. In the mid-1990s, Laura Liswood, a founder of the Council of Women World Leaders, interviewed 15 women presidents and prime ministers. "Most women will articulate that they are over-scrutinised," Liswood told me. "That is what the women I have talked to, the presidents and prime ministers, said. They are over-scrutinised not only for their dress, but in terms of their competence and abilities." The harshest critics were often other women. Schroeder had women mailing her style tips – and cheques so she could get her hair done. Moseley Braun provoked a revolt among women staffers when she turned up at the Senate in 1993 in what she describes as a conservative black trouser suit. No female staffer was allowed to wear trousers. Other women leaders encountered profound outrage among some women that they had dared to play in a male arena. "They figured that if I were doing a man's job – the second most important job in the world as vice-president of the United States – their husbands would look at them and say, 'What are you doing?' and they would suffer by the comparison," Ferraro said. "They felt that their jobs at home as wife and mother were probably not that important."

WHY DON'T YOU
LOOK LIKE A LEADER?

Pat Schroeder argues that Americans simply cannot
conceive of what a woman president would look like. "It is
still really hard for women to have that working image that
men have. We know what they do. They loosen their tie
and collar, and throw their jacket over their shoulder. They
run down steps or something. They talk on a cellphone. If
they want to look tough, they play touch football."
Women, she says, don't even have a "uniform" for politics,
unlike men with their "red tie, white shirt, blue jacket".

"The script hasn't been written yet," agrees Moseley
Braun. "The visuals don't exist for a woman in leadership."
Perching on a stool during a debate might allow male
candidates to look casual and relaxed, she said; for women,
it is a nightmare of worrying whether their slip is showing.
"During the debates, for example … all the candidates step
out on the stage and do a raised-arm victory salute. For
fellows to raise their arms over their heads onstage is a
good thing. For a woman it is a problem."

American voters have also become accustomed to
seeing pictures of would-be presidents engaged in an
array of manly leisure activities, all designed to demonstrate that at heart they are just ordinary folk. It's
unlikely, however, that we will ever see a photograph of
Hillary Clinton throwing a football, or putting on waders
to stomp around a marsh shooting ducks. We definitely

won't see her windsurfing, or doing anything else that involves a swimming costume – not after paparazzi captured her from the rear on a beach in the US Virgin Islands in 1998. Clinton's favourite outdoor pursuit is walking, and when she wants to de-stress she cleans out her closets – decidedly not photogenic.

DO YOU HAVE THE EXPERIENCE?

To non-Americans, the system of selecting a president – or a presidential candidate – can seem impenetrable. Unlike in many countries, elections have a fixed date – the first Tuesday in November every four years. The president is elected not directly by popular vote, but by an electoral college, with each state having one elector for every member of Congress. The District of Columbia, which is not fully represented in Congress, has three. The candidate who secures 270 of the 538 electoral college votes wins – even if he or she loses the popular vote.

Democrats and Republicans choose their candidates at a ballot of delegates to a national convention, which is typically held the summer before the presidential election. In the run-up to that convention, states hold primary elections or caucuses to choose which delegates to send to the convention. Primary elections are just like general elections, with voting by a secret ballot. All eligible voters can take part in the primary process, but they can only vote in one party's primary. States that hold caucuses typically convene a number of meetings where voters gather to decide who to support.

Over the years, the nominee has emerged earlier and earlier in the election season as states advance the date of their primary or caucus to try to exert greater influence over the nomination process. Campaigning now begins almost two years before the presidential election, and a year before the first votes are cast in primary elections. Often one candidate will have commitments from all the delegates needed early on, reducing the convention to a formality. All of which means that aspirants need to raise large sums of money quickly.

Although Iowa traditionally holds the first caucus and New Hampshire the first primary election, a number of states challenged their primacy in the 2008 elections. The struggle led to confusion over the election calendar.

Some argue that America's two-party system has made it impossible for several women candidates to stand at the same time, unlike a parliamentary system, where there can be any number of women running for high office. And countries that practise proportional representation (PR) – rather than the first-past-the-post system of, say, Britain – are even more open because PR more easily allows for affirmative action policies, or "zipper lists" that alternate male and female candidates. Proportional representation also makes it easier for outsider candidates to break through.

Another virtue of a parliamentary system is that it allows women to rise gradually through the ranks over the years, burnishing their résumés and gathering support from fellow legislators. It took Margaret Thatcher 20 years to reach the top after she was first elected to the British parliament in 1959, serving in the cabinet and as leader of the opposition, before she became prime minister in the 1979 election. Elizabeth Holtzman, who spent eight years in Congress before winning election as Brooklyn's first woman district attorney, argues that there is simply more resistance to voting in a woman to a position where she will wield power singlehandedly. "It is still hard in this country for people to accept a woman in an executive position. A legislative position is easier because it's really a lot about talking, and people think women can do that."

* * *

To date, there has only ever been one true test of a woman's electability at the national level – the 1984 elections when the Democratic candidate for president, Walter "Fritz" Mondale, chose Geraldine Ferraro as his running mate against Ronald Reagan and George Bush Sr.

Mondale needed to make a bold move to energise a languishing campaign. He wasn't necessarily looking for a woman deputy – the white Minnesotan had considered an African-American and a Latino man. But Ferraro, then 49, was glamorous, and her life story was the incarnation of the American dream. The US-born daughter of poor

Italian immigrants, she was educated by nuns, had worked her way through law school at night, and raised three children before running for Congress. Ferraro jumped at the chance to make history.

"The only calculation I had to figure out was: was I willing to give up my congressional seat? Which I was. That was the only factor that moved in there – other than if indeed something were to happen to Fritz, could I run the country? Yeah, I think I could," she told me. That calculation that there could be little downside to running was hopelessly naive. It was not long before rumours began to circulate that Ferraro's husband, John Zaccaro, a real estate developer, had Mafia connections, owed thousands of dollars in back taxes, and had raided an elderly widow's trust fund. In 1985, Mr Zaccaro pleaded guilty and was convicted of real estate fraud. He was sentenced to 150 hours of community service and lost his real estate licence for 90 days. Throughout the 1984 race, Ferraro was compelled to devote time when she should have been campaigning to defending her husband. She denied that he had links to the Mafia, and claimed the charges against her husband were politically motivated. And it got uglier. Reagan called her a token. Barbara Bush, the wife of her opponent, all but called her a bitch, coyly rhyming the word off "rich". George Bush himself was not above getting his hands dirty. The day after a heated vice-presidential debate, in which Ferraro went on the offence and accused her opponent of seeking to patronise her, Bush told a group of longshoremen in New Jersey that he had "tried to kick a little ass". Anti-abortion activists called the pro-choice Ferraro a baby-killer. Even Italian-Americans turned against her.

More than 20 years later, Ferraro remains convinced that the White House orchestrated a dirty tricks campaign against her at the personal instigation of Nancy Reagan. Soon after the Democratic convention, the Mondale-Ferraro ticket had a brief surge in the polls. "Nancy Reagan was the one who said, 'We are going to get that woman,'" Ferraro said. "She was looking at the polls when I got the nomination and they thought all of a sudden that they could lose."

In the event, Mondale and Ferraro barely touched Reagan. He was re-elected by a landslide. But for Ferraro, her campaign should be remembered for recruiting thousands of women into Democratic politics, and for paving the way for future generations of women candidates – like Clinton, whom she strongly supports. "I do think that the campaign made a difference," she said. "Pollsters have told me. I have been told that by political analysts who have looked at where women are, and how they have moved. I have been told that by individual women who have stopped me in the middle of the street and said it made a difference in their lives." But it would take more than 20 years for another woman to emerge – by way of Yale law school, Arkansas, the White House and the US Senate – to test just how much America had changed.

PART TWO

FINDING HER WAY

The law student who turned up for work at the legal aid office was dressed in purple from head to toe. She had long brown hair parted severely down the middle, big aviator glasses, and wore purple hip-hugger jeans and an embroidered sheepskin coat, which was also purple. It was, even for Yale University in the early 1970s, a memorable outfit. "She was what I would describe as a vision of purple," said Penn Rhodeen, a legal aid lawyer in New Haven, Connecticut.

The woman was Hillary Clinton, or Hillary Rodham as she was then known. The case on which she was to assist Rhodeen would give her practical experience in an area of the law that she hoped to make her life's work: the protection of children. Clinton, then in her second year at Yale law school, had been studying under a psychiatrist at the Yale Child Study Centre who specialised in children suffering from trauma and neglect. That in itself struck

Rhodeen as unusual. Other women her age were running as fast as they could from anything to do with children and family, but Clinton had steeped herself in the material. She came to the meeting prepared. "She had unusually well-formed ideas. I was really impressed," said Rhodeen. "I felt I was ahead of the curve, but she was already there."

Across the country, students were marching to end the war in Vietnam. Just off campus, tanks circled the New Haven courthouse ahead of the murder trial of Black Panther activists. Peace tents sprouted in the Yale quad, and manifestos splashed across the walls of dormitories. Some of the women at Yale with Clinton were working to legalise abortion in Connecticut. (Such challenges would lead in 1973 to the landmark Roe v Wade Supreme Court judgment that made abortion a right across the country.) Many joined consciousness-raising groups. Those causes did not engage Clinton. She had her law school activities, and her work on children. "There was a seriousness of purpose. It was almost like a calling: how do you use this big system to get this done? And that was kind of brave, because that wasn't very fashionable," said Rhodeen. The two spent six months trying to get the courts to set aside the usual bureaucratic procedures and allow a middle-aged African-American woman to adopt the two-year-old girl she had fostered since birth. They lost. But Clinton thought she had found her purpose.

When Hillary Clinton arrived at Yale in the autumn of 1969, she was confident and exceptionally intelligent, one of 235 high achievers to enter the law school that year. "All along everyone knew Hillary was going to do something. She was serious when a lot of people were pretty darn cavalier," said Susan Godshall, a classmate of Clinton's at Yale who is now a senior vice-president of the New Haven chamber of commerce. "She didn't do a lot of hanging around."

That sense of direction led Clinton to the Child Study Centre. She delayed her graduation by a year to 1973 to sit in on sessions with therapists and classes at the medical school, beginning a lifelong association with leading advocates for disadvantaged children. It is impossible to know where that interest in children's rights might have led her because it was also at Yale that she met Bill Clinton. Their meeting was to have a far greater influence on her life than any of the ambitions with which she arrived at law school.

It is, for many Americans, virtually impossible to look at Hillary Clinton without also seeing Bill. Or, perhaps, the absence of Bill: Hillary famously lacks her husband's outsize personality and easy charm. Even after Hillary had put in years of hard work in the Senate, during which Bill did his best to stay out of the limelight, it remained difficult for the public to see the two as separate and distinct entities.

For better or worse, in sickness and in health, despite months of solo campaigning, Hillary Clinton was viewed by many Americans through the prism of her marriage to

Bill. This was not just about the closeness or distance within their union – although that too continued to be a subject of obsessive interest. (In 2006 the New York Times published a lengthy piece totting up how much time on average the Clintons spent together. It was about 14 days a month, well before the election campaign got under way.) The choices Hillary Clinton had made throughout her marriage, and might continue to make if she were elected to the White House, were a source of perpetual fascination.

As a baby boomer, born two years after the end of the second world war, Hillary Clinton was a fully participating member of a generation that tried to redraw the boundaries of working and family life. *The Feminine Mystique,* Betty Friedan's treatise on the drudgery of housework and childbearing, was published when Clinton was 16 years old. At Wellesley, one of the best women's colleges in the country, and then at Yale, she was trained to compete on an equal footing with men and to pursue a high-powered career in Washington or New York. "Our generation was quite clearly a cusp generation," said Emily Spieler, who graduated with Clinton in 1973 and is now dean of the law school at Northeastern University. "Our expectations of ourselves were different from the expectations of women five or six years older. The women who were five years younger were past that and had a different approach."

Like Clinton, several of the women who were at Yale law school in the early 1970s married within a few years of earning their degrees, and soon faced the difficulties of juggling professional ambitions and family life. But in a decision that continues to confuse or irritate some of her fellow boomers, Clinton followed her husband to the provincial backwater of Arkansas. She spent the next quarter-century trying to preserve her own identity, as wife of a governor in a sleepy southern state, and as the first working woman to serve in the highly ritualised role of First Lady.

"She was setting a path for herself, but it was always in his shadow. He was always the dominant figure. I don't say this to mean that she was a shrinking violet. He occupies all the space in a room. He inhales all the oxygen. I don't think it would matter who she was. She just couldn't compete with him in terms of charisma, and in terms of having a dominant personality," said a contemporary of the Clintons at Yale.

When her husband became president, Hillary Clinton's struggle to define herself on her own terms became highly public, and she was judged harshly for it. Her efforts at self-assertion all too often seemed to touch a raw nerve, and that nerve was re-exposed when she began running for president.

Some of her attempts to find herself involved issues of basic identity, which for Clinton seems to have been an elastic concept. In more than 30 years of marriage, she has used three versions of her name, adjusting identities to political calculation. She was Hillary Rodham for the first five years of her marriage; Hillary Clinton for the next 10 or so, after political consultants told her that keeping her own name was hurting her husband's election prospects in Arkansas; Hillary Rodham Clinton for 14 years once her husband was elected president, and Hillary Clinton again after launching her own campaign for president in 2007. Her official Senate website continues to use the name Hillary Rodham Clinton.

It was hard not to be confused, both by the name changes and the opacity of Clinton's public persona. She had never been at ease talking about herself in public. That same contemporary of the couple at Yale remembered being seated near Hillary while Bill delivered a speech in which he talked about his difficult upbringing. This was when Bill Clinton was governor of Arkansas. "Hillary whispered to me that she was amazed at how revealing he was," the contemporary said. What was natural reserve calcified during the 1992 elections when Bill was running for the White House. Hillary found herself a favourite target of her husband's opponents. The protective layer became a matter of political survival. Soon it seemed she didn't even let her guard down in private, or at least not to her mother. "I don't talk to Hillary about anything deeply personal concerning her marriage," Dorothy Rodham told the biographer Gail Sheehy in 1998. "We don't sit down and have those mother-daughter discussions about how she relates to her husband, her daughter, or anything else as far as her personal life is concerned. We don't talk about deeply personal things." The interview took place not long after the story broke of Bill Clinton's affair with a White House intern named Monica Lewinsky. Dorothy Rodham may have been trying to spare her daughter further humiliation by fobbing off a reporter. Or not.

Clinton grew extremely sensitive – paranoid, her critics would say – about the risks of any disclosure that had not been scrupulously vetted, shaped and controlled. Maintaining that control in a notoriously gossipy town like Washington was a rare accomplishment. Clinton owed the preservation of that code of silence to a team of trusted advisers. Together since her days as First Lady in the early 1990s, they were almost all female, deeply loyal and ruthless in their practice of *omerta*. They went by the name of Hillaryland, and even had T-shirts printed with the nickname. As a number of journalists have ruefully noted, they are the purveyors of the official history of Hillary Clinton. Ask the members of Hillaryland what she is really like and the answers come back strangely consistent. She likes to laugh; she is committed to the Methodist faith of her upbringing; she is considerate to a fault; she is a voracious reader – though it's rare that anybody volunteers the title of a recent book that she has read and enjoyed; she has always wanted to serve. She is a good mother. When Chelsea was small, and Clinton had to travel, she left behind scavenger games for her daughter. If that sanitised portrait fails to satisfy, that may be because the life that Americans can glimpse from the outside seems a lot darker and much more complex.

When campaigning, Clinton is fond of describing herself as someone fortunate to have been born in the middle of America in the middle of the 20th century. She was born Hillary Diane Rodham on October 26 1947 in Chicago, and her early years were spent in the comfortable white suburb of Park Ridge, 15 miles north-west of the Loop, the elevated track that delineates Chicago's central business district. It was outwardly a conventional suburban girlhood. Her father, Hugh, the upwardly mobile son of a poor Pennsylvania loom operator, drove off every morning to his curtain-making workshop in town in a new-model Cadillac or Lincoln.

Her mother, Dorothy, stayed home and looked after house and family, which included Hillary and her two younger brothers, Hugh and Tony. Summer holidays were spent back in Pennsylvania, where the young Hillary connected with her father's working-class roots. But home life with this tyrannical man was anything but idyllic. He was swift to criticise, slow to praise, grudging with money and generally cantankerous. During Chicago's arctic winters, he turned off the heat overnight, and in her memoir Clinton describes begging him for weeks to let her buy a dress for her high school prom. (She attended an all-white school, where she excelled at academic subjects.) If Hillary or her brothers left the cap off of a tube of toothpaste, their father would hurl it out of the window, and force them to search for it in the snow. It was meant to be a lesson in frugality, she writes. "Occasionally he got carried away when disciplining us, yelling louder or using more physical punishment, especially with my brothers, than I thought was fair or necessary. But even when he was angry I never doubted that he loved me," Clinton writes in her book on raising children, *It Takes A Village*. Her mother was the source of warmth and support, taking pride in Clinton's seriousness and encouraging her to excel.

But Dorothy Rodham had her demons too. Her parents were teenagers when she was born – her mother was just 15 – and they were immature and apparently neglectful. They divorced when Dorothy was eight and a younger sister three. The two girls were sent to live with their paternal grandparents in California, travelling alone by train from Chicago to Los Angeles. Clinton writes in her memoir that the grandparents mistreated Dorothy and she left that home at the age of 14, working as a domestic to support herself until she finished high school. Dorothy was lured back to Chicago by her mother, who had remarried and promised to support her through college, but the reunion was unhappy. Dorothy moved out on her own and took office jobs to pay the bills. She met Hugh Rodham in 1937, marrying five years later. The hard-luck childhood taught her the importance of knowing how to fight. When Hillary was about four and being bullied by another girl in the neighbourhood, her mother told her to go back out and hit the girl back; it was the only way the two could be friends. She did, and returned home triumphant.

In *Living History*, Clinton describes the awakening that would gradually shake her loose from her father's deeply conservative moorings (her mother was a closet Democrat). The key agent was a Methodist youth pastor, the Reverend Donald Jones, who arrived in Park Ridge fresh out of divinity school the year that Clinton turned 13. Jones drove a red convertible, played Dylan on his guitar, and seemed determined to bring the world outside Park Ridge to his youthful charges. He took Clinton and the other members of the church youth grip into poor Chicago neighbourhoods to meet Latino and African-American teenagers. He showed them a copy of Picasso's Guernica, introduced them to the poetry of EE Cummings, and took them to hear Martin Luther King speak at Chicago's Orchestra Hall. Clinton met King afterwards and shook his hand. Jones proved too radical for Park Ridge and he was edged out of his job two years after he came into Clinton's life. But Methodism was crucial in forming her outlook on the world. The two remained in lifelong contact. When she took part in a presidential forum on faith in 2007, Jones came down to Washington from his home in New Jersey and took a seat in one of the front rows.

Encouraged by two student teachers at her high school, Clinton applied to universities outside the

Midwest, and was accepted at Wellesley college in Massachusetts. She arrived there in the autumn of 1965 as an intimidated teenager who thought she could never fit in, and a reflexive Republican. Her mother's lessons in resilience came in handy again. When Clinton phoned her parents in those early uncertain days, desperately homesick, her father told her she could come home if she liked. Her mother told her not to give up. Clinton stuck it out, and the experience was transformative.

By the time she graduated four years later, many in her generation had been radicalised by the Vietnam war and the assassination of Martin Luther King. Clinton, though nominally president of the college Young Republicans club, was also deeply disenchanted. She was no longer a Republican at heart, although she was definitely not a subscriber to the counter-culture that was sweeping American campuses. She also learned she was a good political organiser. Clinton was elected student president, opening her campaign well before the official start of the electioneering season. She began planning for a career that would allow her to make a difference in the world. Law, she decided, would be the right avenue. As she was deliberating on her future, Clinton gained experience of another kind of leadership – as a voice for her generation. Her classmates chose her as the first student to deliver Wellesley's commencement address on the day of their graduation.

In her rambling, passionate and at times incoherent speech, Clinton tried to describe her classmates' sense of disillusionment and desire for change. "We are, all of us, exploring a world that none of us even understands and attempting to create within that uncertainty. But there are some things we feel, feelings that our prevailing, acquisitive and competitive corporate life, including tragically the universities, is not the way of life for us. We're searching for a more immediate, ecstatic and penetrating mode of living," she said. The address brought her fellow graduates to their feet, and earned Clinton coverage in Life magazine.

Three months later, she arrived at Yale. After four years at an all-women's college, she was one of 27 women in her class of 235 law students. They were raised by a generation of mothers who had never worked outside the home. Some of the 27 told me they had never met a career woman before going off to college. But as students it rarely occurred to them that they might not enter the workforce after law school, or that raising children and other aspects of family life might lead them to give up work. They were not necessarily interested in acquiring rich husbands or jobs at large law firms, they said. They wanted careers that mattered. "I was part of the generation that was intent on saving the world," said Clinton's contemporary Emily Spieler.

For some Yale students, that meant immersing themselves in the causes of the left: the protests against the Vietnam war, the Black Panthers trial, women's rights. Clinton, though interested in politics, was not that kind of activist. A number of her classmates associated her with a cautious and more centrist approach. As Susan Godshall recalled: "She wasn't the sort that would have camped out overnight in the law school courtyard to make the administration change its mind about something. My sense is that she – and there were a lot of people like this – was just less comfortable being on the firing line, out there on the political frontline in a very ultra-liberal kind of way." In those days, student politics at Yale ran the range from extreme left to extreme right. "I think Hillary fell into the middle [group] of people who might have sympathised with the disadvantaged but didn't necessarily feel that she had to be out in front of the tanks," said Godshall.

But it was an anxious as well as an idealistic time. As women students, were they taking the place of someone more worthy, a man who might be sent to Vietnam, or a woman who would study that much harder? "I think everyone was aware that she was taking an important place in an important institution that any other woman would like, and there was somewhat of an obligation to try and use that education for something professional," said Joan Tumpson, who practised law for more than 20 years and now makes her living as an artist. A number of her paintings hang in the Clintons' home. "We had a sense of being extraordinary, but there came with it a whole burden of values from my mother's generation, and from the culture in which I grew up in which women were not professionals." Tumpson said she always felt like an impostor.

Clinton, though, is remembered as a woman who exhibited few doubts. In her early 20s, she demonstrated an ability to think strategically about her future in a way other women her age did not. "In some ways, I think Hillary was more sophisticated than the rest of us. More aware of the possibilities; more directed. She was passionate about issues and causes and steadfastly committed to wanting to leave the world a better place than she had found it," said Judy Harris, another woman at Yale at the same time, who is now a partner in a large firm in Washington. "Hillary has known since day one what mattered to her. She set goals for herself and moved towards them."

Her course changed dramatically during her second year, when Bill Clinton arrived at Yale, following two years at Oxford as a Rhodes scholar. He was tall, fearsomely bright, exuberant, and talked incessantly about Arkansas. His wife-to-be thought he looked like a Viking. The other law students immediately clocked him as a politician in the making. Bill Clinton had missed the first two months of the term to work on a campaign. At first the two took little notice of one another. Hillary writes in her memoir that she made the first move after watching Bill watch her in the law library. "If you're going to keep looking at me and I'm going to keep looking back," she said, "we might as well be introduced. I'm Hillary

Rodham." The couple had their first date in March 1971. Bill brought Hillary chicken soup and orange juice when she came down with a cold, and they were soon spending all their time together. When Hillary went off to a summer job at a leftwing law firm in California, Bill followed her.

They were deeply in love, and spent hours driving around in Bill's battered car talking about their future, but, as Hillary tells it, she was ambivalent about committing to him. She was unsure about their future as a couple, and about the idea of following Bill to Arkansas so he could begin a career in politics. There is no suggestion the couple discussed the possibility of Bill compromising his plans to return to Arkansas for Hillary. The summer of their graduation in 1973, when she was 25 and he 26, the pair took a trip to Europe, but they headed to opposite ends of America on their return. Bill set off for Arkansas to teach law and wait for the right time to run for Congress. Hillary moved to Boston to work for the Children's Defence Fund, then to Washington. One of Bill's former law professors called offering him a job as a lawyer for the congressional committee preparing the case for the impeachment of Richard Nixon. Bill turned it down, but recommended his girlfriend.

Hillary Clinton's work as a lawyer for the House judiciary committee was the sort that opens doors in Washington, especially for someone with a Yale law degree.

Over the summer, she wrote a long legal brief on the offences that might merit punishment by impeachment. More than 20 years later, she referred the memo to her husband's defence team when he faced impeachment for lying to a grand jury about his relationship with Monica Lewinsky. Hillary Clinton interviewed at a number of leading law firms in Washington. But in August 1974, barely two weeks after Nixon's resignation, she packed her bags for Arkansas. Bill was running for a seat in Congress, and she decided her place was with him. If he were elected, she could soon return to Washington. The decision provoked dismay and disbelief among some of her friends.

"It absolutely surprised me," said Gregory Craig, a friend of Hillary Clinton's from Yale who defended Bill at his Senate impeachment trial. "I thought she was someone who was going to have a very successful role in the Washington DC arena, and she had political sense. She was smart. She cared a lot about stuff. She worked hard. She was clearly someone who was going to be at the top of the Washington DC legal community if she wanted to, so I was a little surprised that she went to a smaller pond."

It didn't get much smaller than Fayetteville, Arkansas, where Bill Clinton's campaign was headquartered. It also didn't get much more chaotic than his campaign. The staff were young and inexperienced, frazzled by the effort of trying to keep Hillary from bumping into the women Bill had been dating. Hillary's hopes of making a speedy return to Washington with Bill as the newest member of

Congress from Arkansas soon vanished. He lost the election. But as Hillary told her friends, she loved him. There were other women, and the relationship was often stormy, but the couple believed that theirs was a real partnership.

Hillary had passed the bar exams in Arkansas in 1973 – she failed the DC exam that same year, a rare academic humiliation. She had met the dean of the University of Arkansas law school at a dinner part with Bill in the spring of 1974, and had a standing offer of a job. She arrived in Fayetteville a day before term started, driving cross-country from Washington. To her surprise, it was a relatively easy adjustment. Small-town life in the Ozark mountains was not so very different from her girlhood in Park Ridge, and there were other women at the university who were as educated and sophisticated as she was. One of them, Diane Blair, who was 36 and had also moved to Arkansas for a man, remained close to Clinton until her death in 2000. The work went well. Clinton, who was known as a "lady professor", taught criminal law and procedures, and developed a reputation as a tough and challenging tutor. Her lectures were more tightly bound than her husband's freewheeling discussions on constitutional law, and she was far less forgiving when it came to grading students' work.

The couple married in October 1975 in the living room of their home, which was still being decorated. Hillary Clinton was 27. If she had chosen a traditional path in following her husband's ambitions rather than her own, she bowed to few conventions for the wedding. There was no engagement ring, no engraved invitations, and she kept her maiden name, Hillary Rodham. There was almost no wedding gown; she bought a dress at a local department store the night before. And there was practically no honeymoon. When the newlyweds took a trip to Mexico two months later, the entire Rodham clan came along – father, mother and both younger brothers.

Life in Arkansas began unfolding according to Bill's plan. In 1976, he was elected the state's attorney general, and the couple moved to Little Rock, the state capital. It was less of an easy fit for Hillary. The Reverend John Miles, the Methodist minister who presided over the funerals of Bill Clinton's mother and stepfather, described Hillary as a "duck out of water" in those days. "She was bright and sharp and didn't look like she came from Arkansas – not that people from Arkansas are not bright and sharp. But she was very uptight from our standpoint," he told me. "Hillary was not standoffish, but she was a very private person and thrown into this mixture where Bill knew and loved everybody. She was kind of out of place at the beginning but she ended up wonderfully placed."

Hillary Clinton spent 18 years in Arkansas. When Bill ran for president, it was the longest she had lived anywhere as an adult. Those years were an off-ramp for her ambitions of being a major player in Washington in the world of law or policy. Instead, she became her family's breadwinner, providing the cushion of financial security that Bill's relatively low paid job could not. In 1976 she joined the Rose law firm, the most established practice in Arkansas. Although it would have been politically ill-advised elsewhere for the wife of the state's top law official to practise law at the leading corporate firm, such concerns about conflict of interest apparently did not apply to a backwater like Arkansas.

Two years later, Bill Clinton was elected governor, and his wife was now expected to play a public role as First Lady of Arkansas. She did not warm to the prospect. Hillary, by most accounts, had little interest in trying to look or act like the wife of a southern governor. She had no liking for formal banquets, or for ceremony. She continued to be known by her maiden name. "She didn't look the part of a governor's wife," said JoAnn Miles, the wife of the Clinton family pastor. "I don't know how exactly to put that. Her mother-in-law Virginia took an hour every morning to make up her face, and Hillary maybe washed it and walked out the door. It wasn't important to her how she looked. The content of character became more important to her."

Clinton was also absorbed with her own career as a corporate lawyer, and by the birth of the couple's daughter. Chelsea was born in February 1980, after a difficult pregnancy. Clinton suffered a condition called endometriosis, which can make it harder to conceive. She had her friends at the Rose law firm, the closest being another partner called Vincent Foster, who would follow the Clintons to Washington years later.

However, Clinton was soon drawn directly into her husband's sphere of work when he failed to win re-election following a single two-year term as governor. Bill Clinton was devastated. On election night, he sent out his wife to make the concession speech. Although political commentators have always praised Bill's ability to "take a punch", and bounce back from defeat, on this occasion he was left reeling. It fell to Hillary to plan the move out of the governor's mansion and find a home, and to plot her husband's political comeback. While Bill sank into a depression, Hillary recruited political consultants from New York, and helped draft the strategy that would resuscitate his career. She was the one who absorbed the blow and got back up and kept fighting – even at great cost to herself. After the consultants warned that her decision to keep her maiden name had lost her husband crucial votes, she gave it up, even though it had been crucial to her sense of identity. Hillary Rodham became Hillary Clinton. "I learned the hard way that some voters in Arkansas were seriously offended by the fact that I kept my maiden name," she writes in *Living History*.

In 1982, after the couple returned to the governor's mansion, Hillary Clinton was rewarded with an appointment to chair a committee to raise standards in the local schools, which were among the worst in America. She threw herself into the task, conducting hearings across the state, and drafting a plan to set state standards on class size and curriculum. The reforms also required teachers to pass a competency test, a measure that was hugely unpopular with the unions at the time. A quarter of a century later, many Arkansans remember Clinton's efforts on behalf of schools with something approaching awe. "Her caring, and her intelligence and the ability she has to understand the issues – how can people not see that?" said LaJoy Gordon of Camden, Arkansas. "She brought that programme to our state and it saved our schools. I think she is really by the people, for the people." Clinton too considered the reforms among her greatest achievements.

But the foray into education reform was a detour. Although Hillary was Bill's in-house strategist for his campaigns, and a sounding board for his policy ideas, their roles within the family and in public life were clearly defined. During most of her time in Arkansas, she was focused on managing the family finances, and on trying to build a national profile for herself as a lawyer. Some of these investments landed her in political trouble. Not long before her husband was elected governor, she made a profit of $100,000 on an investment of $1,000 during nine months of playing the commodities market. The huge windfall led to allegations of insider trading. But that controversy paled beside the uproar she would later face over her purchase of a plot of land on the White River in a development called Whitewater. The venture became the starting point for a series of investigations into possible conflicts of interest between Bill Clinton's role as governor and Hillary's as a partner in a law firm, and nearly cost him the presidency.

The original plan behind Whitewater, as hatched by the Clintons' friend and major fundraiser in Arkansas, Jim McDougal, was to subdivide the land for holiday homes and sell the lots at a profit after a number of years. But in 1978, when the purchase of Whitewater went through, rising interest rates were making second homes unaffordable. The Clintons and McDougals opted to hold on to their land and wait out the slump. McDougal, who had served as Bill Clinton's economic adviser during his first term as governor, bought up a financial institution, which he renamed Madison Guaranty Savings & Loan. When Whitewater failed, McDougal tried to cover the losses with funds from Madison. He was prosecuted for fraud in 1984 – and hired the Rose law firm to defend him.

The failure of Whitewater and the collapse of the bank became an issue in the 1992 campaign, and Bill Clinton was accused of putting pressure on an Arkansas businessman to extend loans to the McDougals. After he was elected president, Clinton asked his attorney general, Janet Reno, to appoint a special prosecutor to lead an investigation into Whitewater and the bank's collapse. No evidence of serious wrongdoing by the Clintons was discovered in the Whitewater affair – although 14 other people, including a partner at the Rose law firm and others associated with Whitewater and Madison, were convicted on fraud and other charges. But the open-ended nature of the investigation allowed the independent prosecutor, Kenneth Starr, to look into allegations that Clinton had had an affair with Lewinsky.

In addition to her work at the law firm, Hillary Clinton was careful during her years in Arkansas to maintain a profile outside the state. Some of these activities related to children, such as her seat on the board of the Children's Defence Fund. Her other involvements showed little trace of the idealism of her Yale years. The Rose law firm represented the biggest corporations in Arkansas. Clinton also spent six years on the board of Wal-Mart, the notoriously anti-union retail giant.

In all her years in Arkansas, the division of roles between Hillary as breadwinner and Bill as politician was seriously threatened only once. Despite numerous reports of Bill's affairs, Hillary was determined to keep her marriage intact. But in 1989 Bill Clinton told his wife he had fallen in love with another woman and wanted to end the marriage, according to Carl Bernstein's biography of Hillary Clinton, *A Woman in Charge*. He also had doubts about whether to seek another term as governor. During that unsettled time Hillary explored the idea of running for governor in her own right. She abandoned the prospect after two polls showed that Arkansans simply did not like her enough to vote for her. The couple, conscious that a messy divorce would wreck any prospect of Bill

Clinton reaching the White House, reconciled. In 1990 Bill was re-elected governor by a landslide, and began planning to run for the presidency against George Bush Sr. Whatever ambivalence the couple might have earlier felt in their marriage had gone – although the consequences of Bill Clinton's compulsive infidelity had not.

The 1992 presidential elections required Hillary Clinton to make even greater personal sacrifices for her husband's political ambitions, ones she readily made. There was far more at stake than in Arkansas, and the personal cost to Hillary of her husband's ambitions and his weaknesses were greater too. As the couple began their journey from Arkansas to Washington, she learned that her pride in her professional career would not be seen as a plus in a potential First Lady. She also learned that her experience as a lawyer and an occasional social reformer in Arkansas was not always a reliable guide to the ways of Washington.

At the start of the Democratic primary elections, a nightclub singer named Gennifer Flowers told a tabloid newspaper that she had had an affair with Bill Clinton, and that she had secretly recorded their phone conversations. For many Americans, the story of that scandalous liaison was the first they knew of the Clintons. In an attempt to put the story to rest, the couple appeared together on CBS 60 Minutes, with Hillary Clinton making her debut as her husband's protector. She was the wronged woman, standing up for the man who betrayed her, and hoping to save his presidential campaign. The two clasped hands. Bill acknowledged he had caused "pain" in his marriage, but said the two were still deeply in love.

The appearance on 60 Minutes that night rescued Bill Clinton's campaign, but his wife paid a high price. Her strong performance as her husband's defender made her a target for Republican opponents, and she gave them their opening with an on-air comment that was remarkable in its insensitivity. When the reporter said their marriage looked like a political arrangement, Hillary Clinton snapped back. "I'm not sitting here, some little woman standing by my man like Tammy Wynette," she said. "I'm standing here because I love him and respect him and I honour what he's been through and what we've been through together." The comment made her a hated figure in much of America's heartland, where Wynette was much loved. The singer herself was furious; she had written the song in the third person, and resented being seen as a passive victim. The first encounter with Hillary Clinton had exposed something unsettling: a woman prepared to sneer at the way other people lived their lives, and whose control over her own emotions appeared a little too complete, and a little too calculating. How could she sit there by her husband? Did she really want him to be president that badly?

Weeks later, the impression that Hillary Clinton was out of step with American women deepened with another comment to a reporter on how she saw herself within her marriage. On this occasion, though, the subject was not Bill and his sexual transgressions, but allegations of financial impropriety. In the Clinton marriage, money was within Hillary's orbit. In March 1992 the New York Times ran a lengthy article on the Whitewater development, suggesting possible conflicts of interest in the Clintons' investment. The story broke just two days before Super Tuesday, when eight states were to hold their Democratic primary elections. When asked about the report during a campaign stop at a diner in Chicago, Hillary Clinton reacted with self-pity and scorn. "I've done the best I can to lead my life," she told the reporter from NBC television. "I suppose I could have stayed home and baked cookies and had teas, but what I decided to do was fulfil my profession, which I entered before my husband was in public life."

Biographers Jeff Gerth and Dan Van Natta Jr describe Clinton as incredulous that her remarks would cause offence to stay-at-home mothers. But they were a godsend for the Republicans. Clinton was called the "Lady Macbeth of Little Rock", and the "Winnie Mandela of American politics". Polling revealed that she was a drag on her husband's electoral prospects, and a memo went out from senior campaign advisers: keep Hillary Clinton away from the cameras. She went into retreat. The woman who re-emerged in late spring was a different Hillary Clinton. She was an enthusiastic baker of cookies, challenging Barbara Bush, the wife of her husband's Republican opponent, to a recipe contest sponsored by a women's magazine, and spent her time reading stories on camera to young children, or cutting the ribbon at the opening of new campaign headquarters.

The 1992 elections were, among other things, a contest of class and generation. George Bush, who was seeking re-election to a second term, was the scion of a privileged family who had served as a fighter pilot over the Pacific during the second world war, been elected to Congress and headed the CIA. He was 68. At 46, Bill Clinton never knew his biological father, who had been killed in a car crash a few months before his birth, and he carried the surname of a stepfather who was violent and a philanderer. Clinton would learn only after his election as president that his biological father, William Jefferson Blythe, had at least three wives before his mother, and had fathered and abandoned a number of other children. Bill Clinton also lacked Bush's military record. He had avoided going to Vietnam, and his political career had been confined to Arkansas. The battle lines spilled over to their wives: the white-haired Barbara, who had never worked outside the home, and successful lawyer Hillary.

In her memoir, Hillary offers her take on why she might have been such a consistent target of hostility. "While Bill talked about social change, I embodied it. I had my own opinions, interests and profession," she writes. "I represented a fundamental change in the way women functioned in our society." Hillary Clinton arrived in Washington determined to bring that change to the role of First Lady. She wanted to turn the largely ceremonial position into a role that would be commensurate with her experience as an Ivy League-educated corporate lawyer, even after she was forced to abandon her hopes of formally serving as her husband's White House chief of staff.

Other First Ladies had played an active role in their husband's administrations before Clinton. After Woodrow Wilson was left partially paralysed by a stroke in October 1919, his wife, Edith, all but ran the country – although she made certain that nobody suspected how incapacitated he was until years afterwards. Eleanor Roosevelt, whom Clinton has often cited as her heroine, wrote a weekly newspaper column and was active in the civil rights movement. Rosalynn Carter sat in on cabinet meetings. Nancy Reagan, who had worked as an actor before her marriage to Ronald Reagan, insisted that astrological charts be read before scheduling his public events, and had frequent clashes with his chief of staff, Donald Regan. As for Barbara Bush, she may have cultivated the image of a kindly grandmother, but she exerted strong influence on decision-making, and had no qualms about wielding the hatchet against opponents on the campaign trail.

But a First Lady must always remember her place. "The position of First Lady is a derivational position. You only have it by virtue of your marriage. You have not achieved it on your own," Melanne Verveer, who served as Clinton's chief of staff in the White House, told me. "It's hard for any woman, but she was the first professional woman in that position." Tradition dictated even in the waning years of the 20th century that a First Lady serve as a gracious hostess of state banquets and accompany her husband to public appearances at home and abroad. If she was going to exercise power, it was best to do it discreetly – no titles, no overt display of a veto on cabinet appointments. That went against the grain for someone like Hillary Clinton, who had prided herself on her professional credentials, and had never demonstrated much interest in personal appearance or decor. Before they even got to the White House, the Clintons dreamed of remaking the position of First Lady into one big enough for Hillary. She would be a co-president; or, as Bill joked during the campaign, the voters would get two for the price of one. But as Hillary discovered, that was not how the job worked.

The Clintons' first days in the White House were awkward and confrontational as the new First Lady struggled to prove that she was different from the women who had come before her. She moved almost immediately to reclaim her maiden name after more than a decade of disuse, issuing instructions that she be announced as Hillary Rodham Clinton at her husband's inauguration. A day later, the White House said she would have her own office in the West Wing. It was a clear break with tradition;

no First Lady before had placed herself in the corridors of power. Hillary Clinton's premises in the West Wing were small and uncomfortable. Her staff had to stay in a separate building. But Bill intended his wife to play a central part in his presidency. A few days later, she was entrusted with the signature goal of his election campaign: the establishment of a system of universal healthcare. Had it succeeded, the initiative would have had an impact on the lives of millions of ordinary Americans. In Hillary Clinton's hands, it was a total failure.

It was not that she over-reached, or was striving for too radical an overhaul of America's healthcare system. Hers was not a failure based on boldness, or dewy-eyed idealism. Hillary Clinton dismissed out of hand the Canadian or European models under which the government would insure everybody directly, assuming that Americans would never accept that degree of government involvement. Instead she chose to rework an existing system that relied on employers to offer health insurance to their workers, but which, in those days, left more than 35 million Americans without coverage. The result was a proposal for a combination of government controls and private insurance that was staggering in its complexity.

The conventional thinking would not necessarily have doomed Hillary Clinton's plan to failure, had it not been for her righteous certainty that admitted no room for error, an insistence on secrecy, a failure to understand the political culture of Washington. She made it plain to a number of senators that she intended to "demonise" anyone who opposed her healthcare strategy. The display of vindictiveness instantly racked up a number of new enemies. Under Clinton's leadership, the presidential task force on healthcare grew into a bloated bureaucracy employing 500 experts. The consultants met in such a conspiratorial atmosphere that participants were banned from taking notes. When they did emerge from their seclusion, their plan ran to more than 1,300 pages and was impenetrable. It was no surprise that the Clinton administration's attempt at healthcare reform was attacked by the Republicans and the health insurance industry. What sank it, however, was Hillary Clinton's inability to build support for her proposals from a Democratic Congress. She rebuffed suggestions from outside experts and even Democratic senators, failing to realise that she would need their support to carry the legislation. The healthcare plan collapsed. Two months later, in November 1994, the Democrats lost control of both houses of Congress in the midterm elections.

Hillary Clinton had suffered the most crushing defeat of her adult life. Her intelligence and capacity for hard work, which had served her so well in the past, had been overwhelmed by failings of character. She had demonstrated a tin ear for politics, trying to do too much on her own authority and in secret without taking time to understand the terrain in Washington. Her failure – and the heavy-handedness that contributed to it – had damaged her husband's administration at a critical early stage of his presidency. Her unwillingness to consider a more radical approach to the problem of healthcare, along the lines of the state-backed systems in Europe, has arguably limited debate over reform ever since. It also left permanent scars on Hillary Clinton. Although her plan collapsed because of a failure of execution – not because it was too radical for America – she saw the experience as a lesson in the dangers of adopting policies that advocated wholesale change. She became a devotee of a cautious, incremental approach that she came to call the "school of small steps".

The experience left her deeply shaken. The months of struggle over healthcare had also been a time of loss at a personal level. Her father died in April 1993. In July Vincent Foster, the friend from the Rose law firm who had been brought to Washington as the deputy counsel for the White House, killed himself. A gentle and courtly man, he had found it difficult to adjust to the vitriolic nature of public debate in Washington, especially during the backlash against the Clintons' sacking of an inhouse travel agency. He was also saddened by his lack of access to his former law partner. Clinton was consumed with remorse and guilt.

It was time for her to reflect, to find her bearings again. She shut down her office in the West Wing, and announced a period of self-exile. She renounced her idea of being a recognised power in the White House. "My first responsibility, I think, is to do whatever my husband would want me to do that he thinks would be helpful to him," she told the US News and World Report in February 1995. "It may be something of great moment, but more likely it's just to kick back, have a conversation, or even play a game of cards and just listen to him ruminate."

It was, if not surrender, then a tactical retreat to the comfort and security offered by her circle of ferociously loyal aides. Hillaryland was arguably the most important legacy of her years as First Lady. In a transient city like Washington, such constancy was rare. But Hillaryland operated by different rules even in its earliest days, according to Patrick Halley, a lawyer from Massachusetts who was one of its few male members. It was more collegial, less given to backbiting, and staff felt valued. "She developed a sense that she needed to be able to rely on a category of people close to her who knew what she was doing and had her interests at heart," Halley told me. He spent more than a decade as Hillary Clinton's advance man, scouting out the logistics of her travel.

Loyalty went in both directions. By the start of his second term as president, Bill Clinton had experienced almost a complete changeover of staff. Hillaryland was stable. At a lunch in Little Rock in 1996 to mark the success of Bill Clinton's re-election campaign, all but one of the founding members of Hillaryland sat at the table. Hillary Clinton is famous for remembering the birthdays and anniversaries of her staff, and asking after elderly parents. She took on one speechwriter when she was pregnant with twins, and has seen other members of Hillaryland through cancer and divorce. "Once she decides she trusts you and you are worthy there is a deep sense of commitment," Halley said.

After the healthcare fiasco, Hillaryland was Clinton's sanctuary. She used the space not to remake the job of First Lady – as she had tried and failed before – but to figure out how she could make herself fit into the role without giving up too much of herself. She started by embracing the traditional duties she had formerly disdained, serving as official hostess at home and goodwill ambassador abroad. She wrote a saccharine homily to the importance of raising secure and happy children, *It Takes A Village*, and another book that somehow managed to be even more bland about letters written to the White House pets.

Clinton had not, in fact, morphed into a national Stepford Wife, but she was becoming more politically savvy and, above all, cautious. At home, she remained a potential liability to her husband because of her earlier performance as First Lady. Abroad, there was relative freedom. In September 1995, Clinton attended the UN conference on the status of women in Beijing, and delivered a strong condemnation of female infanticide, rape as an instrument of war, forced abortion and sterilisation. The speech was also a rebuke to China, with its call for freedom of expression and assembly. "It is time for us to say here in Beijing and for the world to hear that it is no longer acceptable to discuss women's rights as separate from human rights," she said.

The conference showed Clinton the way forward. She became the most-travelled First Lady in history, visiting more than 80 countries, and immersing herself in issues from the use of micro-credit in Bangladeshi villages to the oppression of women under the Taliban. Unlike her husband, who could be counted on to get a new burst of energy from going out and shaking hands, Hillary Clinton thrived on interesting encounters. "If we put her in a room with a group of people for a significant intellectual exchange, that is what rejuvenated her," Halley said. Clinton did not entirely abandon a domestic role as First Lady, or her interest in healthcare, but she adjusted her agenda, taking on smaller projects. In her husband's second term, she convened a series of White House conferences on child development, from infancy to adolescence, and she lobbied effectively for new legislation that made it easier to adopt. She also pressed for investigation into the causes of Gulf war syndrome.

But it took a Washington sex scandal to make Clinton's rehabilitation complete, and to allow her at last to take control of her life. In the official Clintonian version of events, on the morning of January 21 1998 the president woke his wife to tell her about a news report that he had had an affair with a White House intern named Monica Lewinsky. Lewinsky was 22 and had just finished college when her mother suggested she try to get a coveted unpaid summer placement – or internship – at the White House in the summer of 1995. The internship turned into a job, and the affair began that November. By April 1996 senior White House staff sensed what was going on, and Lewinsky was moved to a post at the Pentagon. The affair might have remained buried had not Lewinsky confided in an older colleague at the Pentagon who secretly recorded their conversations, and persuaded her naive young friend to keep a blue dress that had been soiled in one of the encounters at the Oval Office. In January 1998 Lewinsky gave an affidavit to Kenneth Starr, who had spent months investigating Whitewater without incriminating the Clintons. She denied the affair, and so did Bill. In a now infamous press conference, he wagged his finger at reporters and said: "I did not have sexual relations with that woman, Miss Lewinsky." His wife, improbable as it may seem given Bill's history of infidelity, said she believed him.

By now there was a familiarity to the First Family's management of such scandals: Bill Clinton sinned, Hillary Clinton saved. Once again, she reprised the role of the wronged spouse on national television. Once again, her defence of her husband set off a secondary scandal. In her first public response to reports about her husband's relationship with Lewinsky, Hilary Clinton was categorical. There had been no affair. "The great story here, for anybody willing to find it, write about it and explain it, is this vast right-wing conspiracy that has been conspiring against my husband since the day he announced for president," she told NBC television.

The following August she discovered that her husband had lied to her after all. As Lewinsky prepared to testify before a grand jury about their affair, Bill woke his wife early one morning to tell her the painful truth. She writes in *Living History* that she was devastated. "I could hardly breathe. Gulping for air, I started crying and yelling at him, 'What do you mean? What are you saying? Why did you lie to me?' I was furious and getting more so by the second." She was unsure the marriage would survive.

But it was also a time of renewal. Hillary Clinton was about to launch her own political career. In her account of her evolution from First Lady to senator from New York, she had never seriously considered running for political office. Elected politics were Bill's orbit. To her friends, she maintained that public service took different forms, and she was satisfied with her role in life.

By the autumn of 1998, however, the clock was beginning to run down on Bill Clinton's time in the White House, even without the threat of impeachment. No matter how the scandal over his affair with Lewinsky played out, by 2001 he would no longer be president, and Hillary would no longer be First Lady. Hillary Clinton was beginning to review her options, inside and outside her marriage. The Clintons owned no home of their own, and there was nothing binding them to Arkansas. Hillary had ruled out a return to her law practice in Little Rock. She thought about running a university, or setting up a foundation that would promote women's rights and democratisation. She explored the idea of a high-profile post in the international arena, at the United Nations or the World Bank. In that period of deliberation about her future, Charles Rangel, a congressman from Harlem who was one of the most powerful African-American leaders in the country, put in a call to Clinton's staff. Rangel had a tip-off that Daniel Patrick Moynihan, who had represented New York for more than 20 years in the Senate, was about to announce his retirement. According to Melanne Verveer: "It was in the heat of Monica, if I remember, and she said, 'Charlie, I have a few other things to be concerned about at this point' – or something to that effect."

It was not the first approach from New York Democrats. State party officials had been looking for a star candidate to revive the party's fortunes, and had batted around the idea of running for office with Clinton in the past. She had never seemed interested earlier, but Rangel was one of her husband's strongest supporters. As a New Yorker, he also had an additional motive. He knew that Rudy Giuliani, then the Republican mayor of New York, was considering a run for the Senate. Giuliani had many enemies among black New Yorkers because of his refusal to meet black leaders, and a number of high-profile cases in which the city's police had killed African-Americans. Rangel raised the idea again during a trip to the Dominican Republic following a devastating hurricane, and this time he thought he saw a sparkle of interest in Clinton's eye. Not long after that, Bill Clinton asked Rangel whether he thought his wife would run a good race. "I knew I had a candidate," Rangel told CNN on the day that Hillary Clinton took her oath of office.

With her husband tied up in Washington preparing his defence against impeachment proceedings, Hillary Clinton took on a central role in the Democratic campaign for the 1998 midterm elections. To her surprise, her humiliation in the Lewinsky affair had accomplished what all her earnest efforts on behalf of healthcare and women's issues never had. Americans were warming to her. Clinton's approval ratings shot up to 70 per cent. "All of a sudden people said, 'Oh, she was not this calculating woman, this polarising woman,'" said Elizabeth Bagley, who was appointed ambassador to Portugal by Bill Clinton. "People thought it was great what she was doing, getting out and speaking. Her husband would have been the one on the campaign trail if he hadn't been in the middle of the impeachment process. But she was out there, and I think people really respected her for that."

Clinton turned her mind towards the practicalities of seeking a Senate seat from New York. No First Lady had ever run for public office, and running for the Senate in New York was an especially audacious move. No woman had ever been elected to state-wide office there, and Clinton, a daughter of Illinois who spent much of her adult life in Arkansas, had no roots in the region. But there were no seats opening up in Illinois, and Clinton knew she could never get elected in a southern state like Arkansas. New York might be her only chance.

She polled her staff, who were cool, if not openly hostile, to the idea. Members of Hillaryland thought the White House years had already exacted a punishment on their boss. A run for the Senate would wear her down completely. Patti Solis Doyle, who would go on to manage Clinton's presidential campaign, told her flatly she did not think she could get elected in New York. Clinton consulted more broadly. She sought the advice of her husband's White House aides, Democratic strategists in New York, state party officials, union leaders, pollsters and political consultants. She was extremely thorough. "She had many, many, many meetings," said Verveer. "It was a lengthy, lengthy process." In her memoir, Hillary Clinton links her decisions to remain married to Bill and to run for the Senate, and describes them as the most difficult of her life. "With my mind clearer about where I wanted to go with Bill, I felt freer to take the first steps towards a race for the Senate," she writes. After all her deliberations, Clinton realised politics was what she knew best. It was nearly three decades since the young law student with a predilection for purple had turned up at a legal office in New Haven determined to devote her life to working on behalf of children. For nearly all of those years, she had diverted that sense of purpose into building up Bill Clinton's political career. Now it was time to strike out on her own.

PART THREE

A CAMPAIGN OF HER OWN

NEW YORK

There are few places within the boundaries of New York state as far removed from the towering high rises and fast-paced life of Manhattan as the town of Jay. Jay, a collection of hamlets nestled among the Adirondack mountains, lies about 290 miles north of New York City, and has a population of 2,306. There has been no industry here since the paper mill shut down nearly 40 years ago, and people think nothing of driving 50 miles to work. It's the kind of place where Main Street consists of a handful of shops, a bar and three churches, and where the Stars and Stripes are draped above the doorways of wooden houses.

Forget for a moment the outsize tug that is Manhattan. Most of the 19 million inhabitants of New

York state live outside New York City. If Hillary Clinton was going to maximise her chances of being elected to the Senate in 2000, she had to establish a connection with those voters. She needed to build a base not just in the city, and in the Republican suburbs of Long Island, Westchester and Rockland counties, but in upstate New York, directly to the north, and in the area known as the Western Tier. And if she ever hoped to use her record as senator as a stepping stone to the White House – which was a subject of constant speculation – she had to appeal to voters whose daily lives had more in common with the people of Jay than the urbanites of Manhattan.

Clinton had to learn the ways of Congress, if she was going to be an effective senator. She had to ingratiate herself with the same senators who had viewed her as a haughty and difficult First Lady, and she had to learn how to use the levers of government to benefit the people of New York state. That imperative increased after 9/11, when Clinton needed to show she could respond effectively to the task of rebuilding lower Manhattan, as well as meet the needs of rescue workers and other survivors of the attacks. In the smouldering ruins near Ground Zero, as in the rust belt towns and dairy farms of upstate New York, Clinton had to deliver.

Woody Allen, that famous denizen of Manhattan, once said that 80 per cent of success is just showing up. That could have easily served as Clinton's motto, at least so far as it concerned the town of Jay.

On a Saturday morning in April 2002, Jay and surrounding areas of Essex County were struck by an earthquake, a rare occurrence in the Adirondacks. The magnitude was 5.3 on the Richter scale, which was relatively mild. No lives were lost. But it was nevertheless a calamity for a small community. It took a few days for town officials to get the measure of the damage, the compromised structures and wells, but they realised their small budget wouldn't stretch to the cost of rebuilding.

That Tuesday, Tom O'Neill, then the town supervisor, was in his office at the community hall when his secretary told him Hillary Clinton was on the line. O'Neill naturally assumed it was an aide, but when he took the call the senator herself was on the line. "She didn't say, 'This is Senator Clinton.' She said, 'It's Hillary. I heard about the earthquake and I want to help.'"

Clinton reached town that Friday morning, installing herself in a ground floor office of the community hall for a meeting with federal relief officials, town officials and locals. She spent more than an hour at the hall, grilling officials about damage claims and compensation, and hearing from local people about what they needed to get their lives back on track. O'Neill does not remember her taking notes, and was impressed with her ability to remember the names of people at the session hours later. "It was very comforting for people to have their senator in town, and have her say, 'I am going to fight for you, and I am going to help bring things in the town back to normal,'" said Cliff Donaldson, the main administrative official of Essex County. It was Donaldson, who had met both Clintons in the 1970s when he attended a small college in Arkansas, who had suggested the visit to Hillary's local Senate office.

After Clinton returned to Washington, her staff in upstate New York kept in touch with town officials, checking in to see what they might need. On Capitol Hill, Clinton used her power as a senator to steer disaster funds in Jay's direction. The town received $1.16m in relief – about equal to Jay's annual budget – but many people attached equal value to Clinton's effort to make a personal appearance. She was the first major elected official to reach Jay after the earthquake, arriving before the Republican governor of New York state and the Republican representative for the area that includes Jay in Congress. "The fact that she came to such a small hamlet – that probably only has as many voters as one block in New York City – means it certainly was not for gathering votes. That is what was so amazing about it," O'Neill told me.

Tradition had it that the area around Jay was Republican terrain. Clinton lost Essex County to her opponent when she first ran for the Senate in 2000. In 2006, four years after the quake, she carried the county. Being there has its rewards. As John Zogby, a Democratic pollster from the upstate town of Utica, told me, "Clinton gave upstate first and foremost what they were looking for, which was presence. This was not going to be yet another national figure or icon just paying respects at the last minute. This was someone who was going to spend time, who was going to be physically present."

The visit to Jay was a natural progression of a strategy developed by Clinton during her first, successful campaign for the Senate in 1999. The "listening tours" were a series of trips across New York state where Clinton met officials and local people to talk about practical issues such as job losses, healthcare and education. The intense focus on practical politics, on meeting the day-to-day needs of ordinary people, became Clinton's signature. Constituency work was crucial in her evolution from the largely ceremonial role of First Lady to energetic and able senator.

Clinton faced real challenges when, at the height of the Monica Lewinsky scandal, she decided to run for a seat in the Senate. Clinton had never lived in New York state, while the man who was expected to fight her for the seat was Rudy Giuliani, Brooklyn born and bred. A three-time mayor of New York, he was also a tough campaigner. Clinton, in contrast, was not gifted with charisma. Although she underwent hours of media coaching at the beginning of her campaign, she had some distance to go before catching up with Giuliani.

And she had no experience of asking for votes on her own behalf. "It's awkward going from being part of the team to flying solo," she told the Boston Globe during the campaign. "If you were looking for an analogy, I don't know what it might be – maybe like leaving a singing group, where the lead singer is somebody else, and you decide to go out on your own." The article noted that Clinton likened her predicament to that of Al Gore, who had served as her husband's vice-president for eight years before launching his own run for the White House. Both candidates had trouble adjusting to saying "I" instead of "we". Gore, however, had won six elections to Congress, four times as a member of the House of Representatives and twice as a senator, before winning two presidential elections as Bill Clinton's running mate. His political knowledge and skills were easily quantified; Hillary Clinton's were not. She was asking the people of New York to take it on faith that her experience as First Lady had allowed her to absorb enough knowledge of the workings of government to do an effective job.

Charles Schumer, a Democrat who would be her colleague in the Senate if she succeeded, had already set a high standard. Another native of Brooklyn, fearsomely bright and pugnacious, Schumer had won his first election to the New York state assembly straight after graduation from Harvard law school. His arrival in the Senate in 1998 had been an upset, toppling a Republican, Alfonse D'Amato, who was legendary for keeping his constituents happy. Now Clinton was trying to duplicate Schumer's feat.

It was far from clear she could win, even in a heavily Democratic state like New York. Although she had enjoyed a surge in popularity because of her handling of the Lewinsky scandal, she had been viewed as a chilly, calculating woman for much of her time in the White House. Even now, she continued to rub a lot of people the wrong way. Women especially were said to distrust her, and the mere fact that she had acknowledged political ambitions was a cause for additional indignation for some of them. In their eyes, Clinton was an opportunist and a carpet-bagger, out to use New York to further her own ends.

Clinton set aside those doubts. As she told aides when she began her lengthy deliberations about running for office in New York, she believed she could be a force in politics. She cared deeply about healthcare, women's rights, the welfare of children and other issues. She had been involved in politics for virtually her entire adult life. She believed she could use political power in an effective manner. And New York was not an entirely outlandish choice for her electoral debut. A generation earlier, Robert F Kennedy was elected to the Senate from New York. He too used the Senate seat as a base for his run for the White House, until he was assassinated during the Democratic primaries.

Both Clintons were beloved in New York City, which was a Democratic stronghold, and Hillary had made four solo trips to the state in the 1998 midterm elections to campaign for Schumer. State party officials wanted Clinton to run, and New York was a good test run for a future presidential campaign – no matter how much

Clinton denied that was ever a part of her calculation. The state, with its mix of ethnicities in New York City, and its hinterland of ageing industrial hubs, sprawling suburbs and rural villages, was a smaller version of the national political canvas. There was another important consideration: New York City was one of two major fundraising centres for the Democratic party. As an elected senator, Clinton would be near the heart of the money machine.

On July 7 1999 Clinton boarded an air force jet and flew to Binghamton, New York, to make the journey by road to a farm near the town of Oneonta, about an hour's drive west of the state capital, Albany. It was late morning by the time she arrived at her destination, a 900-acre estate belonging to Daniel Patrick Moynihan. Moynihan, a Democrat who was retiring after more than 20 years in the Senate, had been one of the harshest critics of Clinton's healthcare plan. He and his wife and campaign manager, Liz, did not immediately warm to the notion that he would be replaced in the Senate by a former First Lady who had never contested an election. But a key Clinton aide had worked for Moynihan, and eventually won him around. For Clinton, there was little choice but to forget their earlier run-in. She needed to show a semblance of roots in New York, and so she stood by Moynihan's side as the senator, who prized himself on his erudition, delivered a lengthy speech. His endorsement, when it came, was almost as an afterthought.

Right: Hillary and Bill Clinton on their wedding day, October 11 1975. The couple were married in their first house in Fayetteville, Arkansas, the state that would be Hillary's home until 1993

Left: Hillary Clinton as a student at Wellesley College in 1969 as the Young Republican was moving from her father's party towards the Democrats

Above: Hillary with her daughter, Chelsea, as a toddler

Below: Hillary takes the microphone in New Hampshire in early 1992. Her husband's surprise second place finish in the New Hampshire primaries helped carry him to the White House that November

Above: The Clintons take to the dance floor at a Washington ball on January 20 1997 after Bill was sworn in for a second term as president

Below: Hillary poses with Bill and Chelsea and the outgoing vice-president, Al Gore, after her official swearing-in as the Senator from New York on January 3 2001

Above: Clinton takes her place in a row of male opponents at a candidates' debate in New Hampshire in June 2007. She is flanked by her two main rivals, John Edwards (*left*), and Barack Obama (*right*)

Below: Clinton makes a direct appeal for the women's vote in a rally on the west lawn of the US Capitol on April 24 2007, Equal Pay Day

Scores of reporters were watching, and Clinton was visibly nervous. She pre-empted questions about the legitimacy of her standing as a candidate, saying: "Now, I suppose the question on everybody's mind is: why the Senate, and why New York and why me? All I can say is I care deeply about the issues that are important in this state, that I've already been learning about and hearing about." Then Clinton set off on her first day of campaigning as a candidate in her own right, not a spouse or stand-in.

Although Clinton had seemed diffident at the farm, her decision to launch her campaign from upstate New York was bold. Historically, Democratic politicians in the state had relied on their supporters in New York City to vote them into power, spending just a few days campaigning elsewhere. But since the 1950s demographic changes had altered the distribution of voters. New York City was no longer quite the powerhouse it had once been in deciding the fate of politicians. The flight to the suburbs had increased the influence of areas such as Long Island and Westchester county, where voters tended to be more conservative. Upstate New York, where Moynihan's farm was located, now accounted for 40 per cent of the votes cast in New York elections. And while the urban centres of Buffalo, Rochester and Syracuse tended to support Democrats, rural and suburban areas of upstate New York and the Western Tier leaned towards the Republicans.

Democratic strategists, then, understood the importance of trying to win votes upstate. They also knew it could be done. In his 1998 race, Schumer had campaigned heavily across New York state, paying particular attention to the northern upstate region – and the effort had paid off. Now Clinton proposed to borrow Schumer's strategy, but to bill her first swing through the state as a listening tour. "I intend to be spending my time in the next days and weeks and months listening to New Yorkers," Clinton told the reporters at Moynihan's farm. It was a shrewd move.

During the months ahead, Clinton made several swings through New York state, travelling in a two-toned van. She visited school auditoriums, town halls and hospitals, marched in parades, and saw the sights at state fairs. "What Schumer did was really to rewrite the book, but what Hillary did was extraordinary. I assumed Hillary would do what a lot of other people did and assume, 'Hey, I am a Democrat. I need to win New York City big, neutralise the suburbs, and do whatever I need to do in upstate New York.' And that would have been a recipe for failure," the pollster Zogby told me.

Clinton was not a natural on the campaign trail. In her first few months, she was stilted, uncomfortable and, like all newcomers, prone to silly mistakes. Despite never having lived in New York, she claimed to be a fan of the Yankees baseball team, and was immediately accused of switching allegiance for political gain. She said she would march in New York's St Patrick's Day parade – even though it bans gay and lesbian groups. But Clinton eventually found her footing and her confidence, especially in small groups and small towns. That should perhaps have been expected. After all, she was raised in the suburbs of Chicago, and had spent much of her adult life in Arkansas, where the biggest city has a population of 200,000. Upstate New York is also sprinkled with small white clapboard churches, many of them Methodist, which is Clinton's denomination.

Although focus groups and polling revealed Clinton to be a polarising figure, she had an uncanny ability to win people over in smaller settings. Gloria Steinem noted the phenomenon. "When she was running for Senate, I made it a project to take Hillary-haters to hear her speak and all but one of them turned around once they were in the same room as her," she told me. "I wasn't attempting to change people who were polar opposites on issues. I was trying to look at people who otherwise would be her supporters, but were influenced by the public campaign against her." Many of Steinem's converts told her Clinton seemed well informed, and warmer than they expected. The one hold-out, according to Steinem, could not accept Clinton's decision to stay with her husband.

Clinton was meticulous on her listening tours about reading up on local issues, and her appetite for new information was limitless. A few hours after her appearance at Moynihan's farm, she headed off to a forum on education at a local university. When someone in the audience suggested that industry was lagging in upstate New York because the region lacked high-speed internet, Clinton asked him to send her a memo. "She was like a sponge. She would soak up every detail," Tony Bullock, who was chief of staff for Moynihan, told me. After she visited the Buffalo News, Bullock got a gushing call from the editor, full of praise for Clinton's understanding of local politics.

Clinton's studious approach was paying off – at times in unexpected ways. Her listening tours had given her an insight into what mattered to the voters of New York state, and she adapted her campaign accordingly. She made an economic recovery plan for upstate New York the centrepiece of her campaign, promising to create 200,000 jobs in six years by encouraging business investment, especially in the hi-tech industry. She also called for tax credits for college tuition and long-term medical care.

Clinton was hardly unaware of the effect her presence had on small-town America. Outside the elite circuit of high-dollar fundraising events, it is rare to see a senator in the flesh. When Congress is in session, senators spend their working weeks in Washington, DC, and as they face election only once every six years, they are not under constant pressure to get out and meet their constituents. In 1999 and 2000 Clinton was still a First Lady, and there was an undeniable glamour and excitement to her visits to small communities – even among people who thought they loathed her and would never vote for a Democrat. Clinton played off that aura, introducing herself as Hillary and directing staff to inform her when a town official had suffered a bereavement so that she could offer condolences. As she made the rounds of upstate New York, the people she met were invariably charmed. "Personable" – that was the word used most often. "One of the things I noticed was her interaction with people and her willingness to take time and listen to what they had to say," said Donaldson, the Essex County official who had contacted Clinton's office after the earthquake. "That is what so many people want from state and federally elected officials. They want someone who will listen."

In the months after her appearance at Moynihan's farm, Clinton attended hundreds of small-scale events, doled out soup at homeless shelters, and marched in small-town parades. "Her secret to success in New York was all those literally hundreds of small-size meetings and encounters that she had with the voters," Bullock said. "There had to be an awful lot of people who when polled said they didn't much care for Hillary Clinton, but in private thought she was doing pretty good stuff."

But as Clinton soon discovered, in modern elections months of hard work and rigorous preparations can be undone by the smallest of gestures: a heavy sigh or raised eyebrow during a television debate, a moment of anger captured on camera. In Clinton's case, it was a kiss. In November 1999 Clinton travelled to Israel and the Palestinian territories. It was her fourth trip to the region as First Lady but only the first as the presumptive Democratic nominee for the Senate in New York, and the conflict between those two roles put Clinton's candidacy at risk.

Clinton's trip was intended as a tribute to her husband's efforts at Middle East peacemaking. But she also figured that the trip would showcase her star power and help win over Jewish voters and donors in New York state. Instead, the tension between the two roles magnified a misstep in the West Bank, and cost Clinton heavily in her Senate race. At the launch in Ramallah of a US-funded health project for women, Suha Arafat, the wife of the Palestinian leader, Yasser Arafat, set off on a tirade, accusing Israel of using carcinogenic crowd control gas against Palestinian women and children. Clinton raised no objections. When the ceremony was over, the two First Ladies exchanged kisses, and Clinton left.

Photographs of that kiss flashed around the world, and in New York aides for Rudy Giuliani pounced. The Republican mayor immediately called a press conference. "I certainly wouldn't have embraced the person who said it, hugged them and kissed them," he told reporters. "Had I been in a situation like that, I would have objected to it."

Clinton spent months and years trying to atone for that kiss, and undo the damage to her support in New York's Jewish community. The incident taught her an important lesson: the interests of nation and New York did not always coincide. As Clinton later admitted in an interview in Jewish Week, "It was a lesson that I certainly learned, because even though I was there in a capacity that I will no longer have, I want people to know that as a senator from New York, I will look out for and defend the interests of New Yorkers."

As a First Lady, she was formally committed to the foreign policy of her husband's administration, which included peacemaking in the Middle East. As a candidate for Senate, Clinton had to be responsive to the people of New York, and its influential bloc of Jewish voters. About 1.6 million Jews live in New York, roughly 8 per cent of the population, and they are overwhelmingly Democratic – unless there is a compelling reason to switch sides. In New York, Clinton could not afford to be seen taking a centrist position on Israel; she had to demonstrate her support for the Jewish State.

When she began her Senate race she presented an easy target for the pro-Israeli camp because of earlier statements on the Middle East. In May 1998 Clinton had expressed support for an independent Palestinian state. The White House officially disowned the comments. Around the time of her visit to Moynihan's farm, Clinton took steps to court supporters of Israel in New York state, writing a letter to Jewish leaders expressing support for the transfer of the American embassy in Tel Aviv to Jerusalem – in contravention of the foreign policy of the US and virtually every other country on the planet. But, despite Clinton's awareness of the importance of the pro-Israeli vote in New York, the furore over the air-kiss with Suha Arafat appeared to take her by surprise.

It took a full day for Clinton to sort out a recovery plan. At first, she claimed Arafat's comments had been lost in translation. A White House spokeswoman later suggested it would have caused a diplomatic incident to walk out of the ceremony. But over the next months, Clinton made a great deal of effort to make amends. She toured synagogues and community centres from fairly secular Manhattan to the Orthodox Jewish enclave of Crown Heights in Brooklyn. She told audiences she regretted even going to Ramallah, and attacked Palestinian textbooks, saying they taught children to hate. She broke ranks with her husband's administration to express support for clemency for Jonathan Pollard, who was sentenced to life in prison in 1986 after he was convicted of spying for Israel. When it came to light that a fundraiser by a Muslim group in Boston had raised $50,000 for her campaign, Clinton swiftly returned the money. Within a few months of her trip to Ramallah, anyone following Clinton's pronouncements on the Middle East would be hard pressed to imagine that she had ever been a supporter of the Palestinian cause. Indeed, her position on the Middle East was to the right of many Jewish Democrats.

"Her Middle East policy is not so liberal. It's very typically strong on support for Israel and tough on the Palestinians," Steve Rabinowitz, a political strategist with strong links to the Jewish community, told me. "While I am sure she supports a two-state solution, you rarely hear her talk about it. You only hear pro-Israeli, anti-terrorist rhetoric, because it's a safe place to be. While it might not be where liberal Jews are, they sort of forgive her because she is with them on every other issue imaginable."

Clinton's determination to distance herself from her earlier support for Palestinian rights naturally disappointed Arab-Americans, but Republican attempts to capitalise on the episode – including smearing Clinton by saying she supported organisations such as Hamas and Hizbullah – outraged them.

While there were other mistakes on the campaign trail, Clinton also had a great deal of luck. A year after the Lewinsky scandal, the press was now being relatively gentle in its treatment of her marriage, and there had been no further scandals at the White House. But on May 19 2000 she had her luckiest break of all. Less than six months before polling day, Rudy Giuliani, the presumptive Republican nominee, withdrew from the race. His stated reason was a diagnosis of prostate cancer. However, Giuliani was also in the throes of an ugly divorce from his second wife, Donna Hanover, following reports of an affair with the woman who later became his third wife, Judith Nathan. A day after Giuliani's withdrawal, Rick Lazio, a Republican congressman from the suburbs of Long Island, announced he would stand.

Lazio was 42 and handsome, and had a nice-guy image compared with Giuliani, who had antagonised white liberals and African-Americans. But Lazio did not have Giuliani's high profile, and he could not command the financial resources that would have flowed towards the mayor. By the time Lazio entered the race, Clinton had been campaigning for nearly a year. Lazio had to scramble to find staff, and a message for his campaign. In comparison with Clinton's towering presence, he was an unknown member of Congress. Lazio needed to define what he stood for – and that is where he failed.

In the crucial last 10 weeks of the campaign, the Clinton team had a formidable political machine: experienced fundraisers, advertising consultants, strategists and, best of all, Bill, who began making appearances in the state. The turning point came in a televised debate held in Buffalo, New York, that – this time to Hillary Clinton's benefit – delivered one of those moments that can entirely change an election. In one confrontation, Lazio demanded that Clinton sign on in support of campaign finance reform, shoving a paper in her face, and shouting: "Right here! Sign it right now!" In the immediate aftermath of the exchange, the (largely male) pundits gave the debate to Lazlo for his forcefulness. But the people watching in their homes – especially women – saw something different. They thought Lazio was aggressive and a bully, and had invaded Clinton's space. As time wore on, that verdict was reflected in opinion polls: the debate had turned the race decisively in Clinton's favour. As in the days following the revelations of her husband's affair with

Monica Lewinsky, Clinton grew in popularity from being seen as a victim.

On election day 2000, after one of the most expensive Senate election campaigns in history, Clinton defeated her Republican opponent, taking 55 per cent of the vote to Lazio's 43. She won by large margins in New York City, carried Westchester County, and did far better than anyone had dared to expect in upstate New York. Clinton had proven she could win over more conservative voters as well as traditional Democrats. The victory was not as convincing as Al Gore's performance in New York state. He won by a 25 per cent margin over George W Bush. Clinton's majority among Jewish voters was embarrassingly slim – just a few percentage points, according to the exit polls. "For a Democrat who otherwise won, that was rock bottom," Rabinowitz said. But for the first time since her college days at Wellesley more than 30 years before, when she had been elected student president, Clinton had campaigned for office and won. She was a senator.

WASHINGTON

On January 3 2001, with Bill and Chelsea by her side, Hillary Clinton was sworn in to office as a United States senator. There was a real sense of history to the occasion. Here was a First Lady, with her husband, who would be president for just 17 more days, holding the Bible as she took the oath of office. Administering it to her was the outgoing vice-president, Al Gore, who had himself been narrowly denied victory in his bid for the presidency.

But the singularity of the achievement was soon over-shadowed by yet more scandal related to her husband's administration. On this occasion, however, Hillary Clinton played more than an equal part. On January 2 2001, a day before her swearing-in, Clinton received an $8m publishers' advance for the sale of her memoirs. The size and the timing of the deal, barely 24 hours before Clinton would have been bound by ethics regulations forbidding such a payment, made her look greedy at the very least. But the crassness of that transaction paled beside the Clintons' last acts in the White House.

On her last day as First Lady, the Clintons moved two van loads of belongings to the couple's new $1.7m home in Chappaqua, New York. Among them, it emerged, was $190,000 worth of furniture, crockery and art that they had received as gifts. In a bizarre variant on a wedding or baby shower, the Clintons, who had lived in official housing in Little Rock and Washington for all but three years of their marriage, had relied on their friends and admirers to give them a start in their new life. About half of the gifts had arrived during their last year in the White House. After an outpouring of criticism, Clinton said they would pay the givers for $86,000 worth of gifts received in 2000. By that point, of course, Hillary had more than enough cash to hand.

Clinton also had to take the heat for her husband's decision to pardon 140 convicts on his exit from the White House. The pardons had outraged liberals as well as conservatives, and led to accusations that the president had dispensed mercy for political and financial gain. In the most contentious case, Bill Clinton had pardoned a fugitive commodities trader called Marc Rich, who was the largest tax evader in American history. Rich's former wife, Denise, had donated more than $1m to the Clintons and other Democratic causes. She had also given the Clintons two coffee tables and two chairs during their days in the White House.

Other cases reflected as badly on Hillary as on her husband. Her two younger brothers, Hugh and Tony Rodham, were implicated in the pardons scandal. At what should have been one of the proudest moments of Hillary Clinton's life, the newly elected senator was forced instead to disown any knowledge of a deal Hugh struck with a convicted cocaine trafficker and a conman that led to them securing pardons from her husband. Hugh Rodham repaid the funds. Hillary's other brother, Tony, also admitted that he had intervened to obtain an earlier presidential pardon in March 2000 for a couple from Nashville, Edgar Allen Gregory Jr and his wife, Vonna Jo. The Gregorys had been convicted of bank fraud. Tony Rodham had worked for the couple as a consultant, but he denied being paid to obtain a pardon. Among the other controversial characters pardoned by Bill Clinton were four residents of an ultra-orthodox Jewish enclave in New York called New Square, who had been convicted of defrauding the US government of $30m. The New Square neighbourhood had voted in a bloc for Hillary in her Senate race.

The pardons and the heavily laden moving vans were a blot on Clinton's efforts to carry out a seamless transition from First Lady to senator. Unlike her early days in the White House, she was intent on operating within the culture of the Senate which – even at the dawn of the 21st century – revelled in male privilege. But Clinton was determined to blend in. Although she was more famous than most of her 99 colleagues in the Senate, the target of television news crews when she walked down a corridor, Clinton worked to dispel the notion that she was too big for her new job. She adopted the same formula she used on the campaign trail: put in long hours and study the material. Until the 2008 presidential campaign got under way, she rarely missed a vote in the Senate.

She also rarely missed an opportunity to make powerful allies. Accounts of her first months in the Senate invariably describe her as retiring and deferential to her senior male colleagues, the first to fetch coffee in meetings, and the last to speak in them. She used flattery to cultivate the longest-serving senator in the history of the chamber, Robert Byrd, a Democrat of West Virginia, asking him to show her the ropes. She used faith to bond with Republican senators by joining their prayer groups.

(As First Lady, Clinton had belonged to a prayer group including prominent Republican women.)

She was equally careful to establish herself as an ally of the other women in Congress. Not long after her arrival, she invited all the other women senators over to her new home in Washington for a baby shower for a Republican member, Kay Bailey Hutchinson, who had adopted a little girl. Clinton gave her colleague from Texas a signed copy of a book by one of the successors to Dr Spock, T Berry Brazelton. Clinton's solidarity with other women, however, was most evident in her loyalty to the members of Hillaryland, whom she had groomed and promoted from the time she was First Lady to her days in the Senate and her run for the White House.

Clinton's efforts to endear herself to her fellow senators, including those who had been her frequent critics as First Lady, were not merely social. She found common cause with the most unlikely of partners – like the conservative senator from Kansas, Sam Brownback, who is also running for president in 2008. After he apologised during a prayer session for his hatred of her as First Lady, Brownback and Clinton teamed up to put forward legislation to help refugees from sexual abuse, and to protect children from violent video games. As Brownback told the Atlantic magazine, the prayer meeting encouraged him to look again at the woman he had once demonised: "It brought me close to someone I did not ever imagine I would become close to." Clinton worked with other members of the prayer group on legislation. The First Lady who was willing to steamroller opponents to push through her healthcare plan had been replaced by a senator who was equally determined to be seen as a conciliator.

Not all of the recipients of Clinton's charm offensive were impressed. "She has a chameleon-like quality in that she sizes you up and figures out what your needs are, and – as much as possible without getting herself into trouble – she will give you what you need," the doyen of commentators on New York politics told me. Alan Chartock, who runs the public radio station in Albany, had watched Clinton up close since she first ran for the Senate. Others accused Clinton of sacrificing her political beliefs to forge alliances with leaders whose views she probably opposed.

But it was an effective strategy for gaining a foothold in an institution that did not easily yield power to women. In 2001, when Clinton took her place in its ranks, the Senate had only 13 women members – and that was an all-time high. Her appearance in the black trouser suits that were to be her uniform when the Senate was in session caused a minor rebellion among Senate staffers, just as it had for Moseley Braun eight years before. Female staffers were still banned from wearing trousers on the floor of the chamber on the orders of the Republican leadership.

Earlier generations of women had served in the Senate on tolerance – or as stand-ins for fathers and husbands who had died in office. Even as recently as the 1970s, Congress was very much viewed as an old – and white – boys' club. Although the first woman arrived in the Senate in 1922, it would take 70 years before they would be anything more than a token presence. Rebecca Latimore Felton, who was appointed to the Senate in 1922 to take the seat of her recently deceased husband, served barely a day, just long enough to find a male replacement. Until the mid-1970s, a third of the women in the House and Senate were widows of congressmen and senators who had met untimely deaths. It was only in 1978 that the first woman was elected to the Senate, rather than appointed: the Republican Nancy Kassebaum. And she was the daughter of a former governor of Kansas and a one-time presidential candidate.

When Pat Schroeder was elected to Congress from Colorado in 1972, she encountered an institution that had been bypassed by the changes sweeping America in the late 1960s and 1970s. At her swearing-in, the speaker mistakenly asked her husband to raise his hand; some of her male colleagues told her outright that she did not belong – that politics was for people who liked expensive scotch, beautiful women and travel by private jet. Schroeder was 32, with two small children. A number of her female colleagues were unwelcoming, and anxious that Schroeder view them as gender-free vessels. "Half of the women that were there had been elected after their husbands died, and many thought they were carrying on their husband's mantle. For many of them being a woman would denigrate that."

Change eventually did come even to Congress, however, beginning in 1992, the year Bill Clinton was elected. The elections that year offered a rare opening for women. The cold war was over, shifting the focus to healthcare, education and domestic issues, where women were on more comfortable ground. A congressional scandal had forced the resignation of several members of Congress, and the public was not kindly disposed to some of the remaining incumbents. Women were also more motivated to run. The struggle over abortion rights had revived under Ronald Reagan, and the first President Bush had appointed a Supreme Court judge who opposed abortion rights and affirmative action and was accused of sexual harassment by a former aide, Anita Hill. The Supreme Court nominee, Clarence Thomas, vigorously denied the allegations by Hill, and four other witnesses who said she had told them of the incidents at the time. He called the Senate's inquiry a "hi-tech lynching for uppity blacks". The spectacle of an all-white and all-male Senate judiciary committee requiring Hill, who is African American, to give graphic details of the alleged harrassment convinced many women that America's politicians were out of touch with the real world.

That year, more women ran for Congress than ever before. When the new Congress went into session, there were 47 women in the House of Representatives, including 24 who had been elected for the very first time. The number of women in the Senate tripled, from two to six. There were at last enough women coming into the Senate to begin talking about blocs. By the time Clinton began her presidential campaign, there were 16 women in the Senate. Three states – California, Washington and Maine – were represented only by women. In the House, there were 71 women.

Those numbers might have been even higher had it not been for redistricting, and the advantage that incumbents have in raising funds for election campaigns. Since the 1990s re-election rates in Congress have routinely run above 90 per cent. "We have rates of change in Congress like the Soviet Union used to have," Katha Pollitt, a columnist for the Nation magazine, told me. "If you get elected, and you get elected once again, your chances of having a lifetime job, or a job for as long as you want it, are astronomical."

More women in Congress, meanwhile, did not automatically translate into greater strength. Many of those who entered Congress in that first wave in 1992 believed they were representing two constituencies – their own seat and the broader concerns of women, according to a study by the Centre for American Women in Politics at Rutgers University. Though they succeeded in pushing through legislation addressing violence against women and women's healthcare, they admitted it had been difficult to reach consensus with women across party lines. The congresswomen also told the authors of the study that their efforts to legislate for women had at times put them at odds with their party leadership. The lesson seemed clear. Throughout the 1990s, women did not yet have the numbers or the clout to change the political culture, especially in an institution that is run on seniority.

Those limitations on the possibilities for women in the Senate would have informed Clinton's calculations when she was plotting her approach to her new job. It was only after Clinton's re-election in 2006, when Democrats gained control of both houses of Congress, that women rose to positions where they could exert real influence. The Democrat Nancy Pelosi became the first woman to serve as speaker of the House of Representatives, a position that according to the US constitution put her second in the line of succession behind the vice-president, Dick Cheney. In the Senate, Dianne Feinstein became chair of the rules committee, responsible for procedure and maintaining ethical standards. But those changes were still six years away when Clinton first entered the Senate. Those who had predicted Clinton would surface in the Senate as a champion of grand causes were proved wrong. She had a laser-like focus on the needs of New York state, and in her thinking on key issues was much more of a centrist Democrat than a liberal.

Senator Clinton proved adept at avoiding the spotlight where controversial issues were involved. When John Ashcroft, a conservative Republican who opposed abortion rights, was nominated as attorney general in early 2001, Clinton kept largely silent, confining her criticism to a press conference in New York state, rather than Washington, where her remarks would have gained more attention. She did, however, vote against Ashcroft's appointment. Three years later, when the Senate was debating a ban on gay marriage, Clinton was also silent, disappointing gay rights activists, although they were relieved to see that she did vote against the ban.

Clinton's legislative agenda as a senator also aimed to please – or at least not to cause offence. It was, in many ways, the doctrine she had adopted in the aftermath of the healthcare calamity: the "school of small steps". Clinton steered away from major policy initiatives. Her campaign promise to create 200,000 new jobs in upstate New York was set aside. She and her staff realised that as a junior senator she did not have the muscle to push through major economic legislation. So she cut her economic agenda down to size.

In her first year as a senator, she introduced 10 bills aimed at protecting the economy of upstate New York. She resisted attempts from the Pentagon to close military bases, and marshalled her influence as a senator and a former First Lady to foster economic partnerships that would yield small but tangible results.

She touted wines produced near the Finger Lakes in upstate New York to the restaurants of Manhattan, flying a group of chefs up for a tour of the wineries. She sheltered upstate apple-growers from Canadian imports by making it mandatory for fruit to carry point-of-origin stickers. She promoted a loft development in Buffalo, and lobbied to ensure the venues of the 1980 Winter Olympics at Lake Placid were properly maintained in case New York put in a bid for a future games.

Her office organised conclaves between the presidents of local universities and business leaders, and between the heads of technical colleges and major manufacturers. The idea, as she saw it, was to encourage exchanges between academia and the business world, and in a practical way encourage the development of curricula that would help young graduates find jobs. And Clinton continued to travel extensively in the state.

The repeated visits to upstate New York, combined with the small-scale economic initiatives, received prominent coverage in the regional press, and favourable notice even from Clinton's opponents. Clinton also made herself accessible to ordinary New Yorkers at the same time as she shunned reporters. Even after she was elected and re-elected, she set up systems at her regional offices to enable people to meet their senator face to face.

"At first I thought she was using the Senate for what she is doing right now," William Berkman, who owns the bookshop in Jay, told me in 2007. He had not been an early Clinton supporter, but after watching her in the Senate, "she has stepped up a couple of notches", Berkman said. His partner, Karla Oehler, chimed in: "I remember thinking she was making an effort. She never came across as a regular Joe, but maybe sometimes people feel like voting for a competent person – even though they are a Democrat or a woman."

That acceptance was crucial for Clinton. From the early days of her campaign for the Senate in 1999, she faced questions about whether she was secretly plotting to run for the White House. Clinton was vigilant about downplaying the speculation when it surfaced again in the run-up to the 2004 presidential elections when reporters questioned the outsize sums being raised for her Senate re-election campaign.

Clinton did not want to jeopardise her standing in upstate New York or the Senate by being seen as an opportunist. "She was very careful. She didn't want any stories about uppity Hillary neglecting her electoral base because she is too busy running for president," Jeff Stonecash, a political scientist at Syracuse University, told me. "It didn't become an issue that she was a big national figure and not attending to little issues in the state. I do polling for candidates around the state, and I would always hear people make mention of how Hillary was helping out, how she was showing up at fundraisers, how she was really doing the small-scale stuff. I think what she decided to do was to build 2008, and do it very quietly and carefully."

The strategy was also in evidence in her Senate votes. After the episode over her kiss with Suha Arafat, Clinton kept New York's interests uppermost in her mind in the Senate – except they clashed with her presidential ambitions. In October 2002 Clinton voted to give President George W Bush the authority to go to war against Saddam Hussein. The vote angered Democrats, especially the liberal wing, but seen in the context of Clinton's run for the White House in 2008, her reasons for supporting the president became more apparent. Clinton stepped out of her role as a US senator on just one other major occasion, an abortion rights rally in 2005 when she reached out to the pro-life camp. Once again, Clinton appeared to be positioning herself for 2008. Clinton might have gone on with her careful strategy for the Senate, making friends across the aisle, wooing the voters she met on her road trips through upstate New York, and planning for the 2008 elections, if 9/11 had not intervened.

The morning of September 11 2001 was as clear and sunny in Washington as it was in New York. Clinton was still at home when the news broke that a plane had crashed into the north tower of the World Trade Centre. She was in the car being driven to the Senate when the news arrived that a second plane had crashed into the southern tower of the complex. Clinton's first thoughts were for Chelsea, who lived in Manhattan, and in news interviews she described her frantic efforts to reach her – and to keep the news that she had not been able to from

Bill, who was on a trip to Australia. That evening, as the smoke rose above lower Manhattan and the Pentagon building across the river from Washington, Clinton joined members of Congress on the steps of the closed Capitol to sing God Bless America.

As a senator representing New York, Hillary Clinton was transformed by 9/11. Her immediate, instinctive reaction was to announce she was standing by Bush "100 per cent", she told reporters. Clinton offered her support "not only as the senator from New York but as someone who for eight years has some sense of the burdens and responsibilities that fall on the shoulders of the human being we make our president", she told the Senate. She said she felt for Bush on a personal level. "It is an awesome and oftentimes awful responsibility for any person." Clinton was also full of praise for her erstwhile opponent in her Senate race, Rudy Giuliani, or "America's mayor", as he was now called.

The attacks on the Pentagon and World Trade Centre forced Clinton to rewrite her expectations of her job as senator. From now on, she realised, her qualifications as senator, or possible presidential candidate, would be judged not only on her ability to deliver economic benefits to her constituents, but to grapple with foreign policy and military strategy in a world that was about to change.

The day after the attacks, a Wednesday, Clinton and Schumer left for New York. The two senators were instrumental in securing an immediate promise of $20bn in federal money to help clear the site of bodies and debris, and begin the process of recovery. On Friday, Clinton returned to New York again, travelling aboard Air Force One with Bush when he made his first visit to Ground Zero. The next day, September 15, Clinton, visibly distraught, spoke at the funeral of Mychal Judge, the chaplain of the city's fire department, who had been administering the last rites to a firefighter when the south tower came down. "All of a sudden the enormity of the tragedy became very personal," she said. Clinton made three visits to Ground Zero during that first week after 9/11 and introduced a bill in the Senate to speed federal aid to families of rescue workers who went missing in the attacks. In those early days, Giuliani was a constant presence at Ground Zero, leading the drive for a speedy clean-up of the site, and for lower Manhattan to re-open for business as soon as possible. As soon became evident, the drive for life to return to normal came at a heavy price.

In the immediate rush to find the living, and the slow sad search for the dead, thousands of firefighters, police and other rescue workers, who worked at the site for hours at a time without protective equipment, inhaled dust from the wreckage. As medical studies subsequently revealed, almost two-thirds of them suffered a host of lung conditions as a result, ranging from asthma and bronchitis to more severe respiratory conditions.

Clinton was among the first to recognise the dangers in the rubble of 9/11. For a senator who was committed to incremental change, here at last was a grand yet uncontroversial cause. What political risk could there be in championing the plight of the heroes of 9/11? In December 2001 Clinton joined efforts to secure $12m for a medical screening programme for first responders. From that point on, she was dogged in pressing the administration to release funds to track the health of rescue workers, with mixed results. "She really beat the drum on the healthcare issue, on funding for healthcare for the first responders of 9/11 and the other people who had been impacted in that area," said Ester Fuchs, who was a special adviser to mayor Michael Bloomberg from 2002 to 2006. "Clinton was the one who really tipped off the city that they had to be more aggressive on this issue." Clinton was also dogged in the Senate on heading off budget cuts to relief programmes for New York City, but, unusually for a senator, she was not seen by other officials as being excessively concerned with getting public credit for her efforts. This made her friends among New York City officials.

In the November 2006 midterm elections, Clinton might as well have run unopposed. Although the contest was driven by opposition to the war in Iraq, Clinton got off fairly lightly for her support for the US invasion. She easily fended off a primary challenge from an anti-war candidate, securing 83 per cent of the vote. Clinton's strong performance on Capitol Hill and on the ground made it difficult for the state Republican party to recruit a high-profile candidate to stand against her. They turned to a former mayor of Yonkers, a suburb of New York City, called John Spencer. Spencer ran an aggressive campaign, attacking Clinton on terrorism and disparaging her looks. She won the state with 67 per cent of the vote, capturing all but four of New York's 62 counties.

It was exactly the style of electoral onslaught Clinton needed for her next big step. On January 20 2007, the senator from New York ended years of speculation and announced she was indeed running for president. Clinton's apprenticeship was over. She had spent more than six years outside her husband's political shadow. She had twice demonstrated that she could win elections in big urban hubs as well as smaller towns and rural areas. She had learned how to connect with New Yorkers in more intimate settings, and believed she could persuade voters across the country to look beyond the caricature the right had painted of her as a divisive First Lady.

She had also learned how to work the same system that had defeated her as First Lady. A few days after Clinton announced her entry into the presidential race, she invited the college-age son of a policeman who had fallen ill as a result of 9/11 to attend Bush's State of the Union address in Washington. The policeman, Cesar Borja, died of lung failure just a few hours before Bush rose in front of Congress. He was the fifth emergency worker to die after inhaling the dust of the towers, and almost instantly he became a symbol of the forgotten victims of 9/11. "9/11 is not over. It didn't end in 2001," Borja's distraught son told reporters. The young Borja was called to a meeting with Bush, and the White House announced the release of $25m towards medical treatment for first responders. After that piece of political theatre, any remaining doubts about Clinton's ability to manipulate the Senate system for maximum PR advantage were laid to rest.

Clinton had no trail of major legislative accomplishments in the Senate. Her caution prevented that. But aside from her early support for the Iraq war, which became an issue in the presidential campaign, Clinton would not be damaged by her votes in the Senate. She had delivered a credible performance on the Senate floor and in its committee rooms. She had shown she could work amicably with politicians who had been among her most ardent enemies. She had also built her own political machine. Clinton was considered a major draw at Democratic fundraisers – second perhaps only to her husband – and she lent out her Washington home for events on behalf of other Democratic candidates. She was also instrumental in building up institutions that could serve as a Democratic brains trust, and broaden the influence of liberals on the popular discourse. She helped found a new think tank, the Centre for American Progress, which served as a holding pen for future staff on her presidential campaign and presumably the next Democratic administration.

The challenge for Clinton was to transport her successes in New York to a national stage. Did upstate New York reflect the concerns of Americans in the Midwestern heartland? To a limited extent. Was it possible to export Clinton's formula for winning over New Yorkers to 49 other states? Probably not. America was too vast. But Clinton's experiences in her first two campaigns and the Senate would stand her in her good stead when she launched herself into her presidential race. She had won over New York, and some of the most powerful figures in the Senate. Now it was time to turn her attention to Iowa, the first state on the road to the White House.

PART FOUR

TO THE
WHITE HOUSE

Hillary Clinton was working her way through the fairground, waving, shaking hands, autographing baseball caps, and smiling, smiling, smiling when she bellied up to the ice cream booth and ordered a Wonder Bar. It's a half-pound brick of ice cream coated with chocolate and rolled in nuts and served on a stick. Clinton proceeded to dig in, as if it were the most natural thing in the world to stroll through a crowd eating while surrounded by secret service agents. "Vanilla," she said, taking another bite. "It's pure." She moved across to another display, drawn by the silvery handle of a mop. "Yeah, I can just see Bill mopping the floor," someone called out from the back of the crowd. Over at the next booth a man selling drill bits yelled: "Give Bill a kick in the shins, and keep him on the straight and narrow." The crowd giggled and smirked. Clinton smiled as if she hadn't heard either of the men, and moved on.

In the summer before an election year, every serious presidential candidate spends a day at the Iowa state fair. It's a ritual. They show interest, real or faked, in tractors and blue-ribbon-winning livestock. They pause in front of the giant sculpted-butter tableau – in 2007 it was a slightly shrunken Harry Potter beside the regulation full-sized cow. They eat all manner of junk food on a stick, and they spend several minutes posing gamely for photographers through a stream of sweat as they flip pork chops on a giant open-air grill. The homage to country living is meant to demonstrate that a candidate, for all the travel by private jet, the outrageously expensive haircuts, and the battalions of media consultants, remains, deep down inside, entirely ordinary. Preposterous as that may seem, on this Wednesday in mid-August, three presidential aspirants made the rounds – Joe Biden, a Democratic senator from Delaware, Clinton, and Rudy Giuliani, the former New York mayor who was running for the Republican nomination. The next day brought two more of Clinton's Democratic rivals, Barack Obama and John Edwards.

The pilgrimages were a result of a quirk in the US political calendar. For years, the small state of Iowa has exerted over-sized influence on the nomination process by leading the season of caucuses and primary elections that determines a party's nominee for president. A knockout win in the caucuses can make a candidate seem unbeatable, bringing her or him to within touching distance of the nomination straight out of the gate, while a loss can destroy them by raising doubts about electability. Iowans – or at least the small fraction of the population that gets involved in the caucus process – take their responsibilities seriously. They want to see the candidates – not just in scripted television debates, but moving among them. They see themselves as arbiters of electability, weeding out those aspirants who are ill equipped to face the electorate.

Winning over Iowans has been a crucial test for every candidate since the 1970s, but Clinton faced bigger challenges than most. She needed to persuade voters that a woman could win a presidential election, and that, despite a reputation for coldness and lack of charm, she was the strongest of the Democratic candidates. She also had to lay to rest nagging doubts about her authenticity. Spending a few hours at the state fair, gobbling up ice cream and caramel apples, was one thing. That was about appearance, the kind of harmless stagecraft all politicians indulge in. Repackaging a personality as well known as Clinton and transforming the public's perception of her core beliefs was an entirely different matter. Those doubts about her authenticity, as much as gender, were Clinton's big liability on the campaign trail.

A few nights after entering the presidential race in January 2007, Clinton pulled out the line she had used to such great effect in her New York races and told NBC television: "I'm probably the most famous person you don't really know." It seemed personable, friendly. She was asking for a second chance. But there was something unnerving about the inability of Americans to get a clear fix on Clinton's politics after she had spent so many years on the national radar, and gone before the electorate twice. What did she stand for? What kind of president would she be? To what extent were her views of the world shaped by Bill Clinton? Would she be carrying on the legacy of her husband's administration, or charting a course of her own?

Since her days as First Lady, Clinton has inspired strong feelings, and a substantial share of voters, around 40 per cent, continue to view her with attitudes that range from vague dislike through deep mistrust to downright hatred. As a senator, though, and on the campaign trail, she has been guided by caution and compromise. The risk-averse strategy has kept Clinton from championing bold ideas or adopting causes that do not have existing support. She swims with the current. The strategy is an adaptation of her husband's playbook of reaching for centrist voters even at the expense of hardcore liberal support. The approach helped Hillary Clinton win election to the Senate and boosted her in the polls in the presidential race, but also caused confusion and mistrust.

Her attempts to position herself in the centre seemed driven by a desire to win the next election, not to reshape the philosophical underpinnings of the Democratic party. In 2002, had she set aside her better instincts to vote in favour of the war in Iraq? Many Democrats on the left wing of the party believed she had, and that that vote foreshadowed how she would function as president and commander-in-chief.

Critics accused Clinton of serving her own narrow interests in voting to give George Bush the authority to go to war against Saddam Hussein. They argued that Clinton was so concerned that she not appear weak or wavering that she had disregarded any information that would cast doubt on the rationale for going to war. In particular, she ignored the urgings of a senior senator and neglected to read the most authoritative intelligence report available on Saddam Hussein's weapons programmes. Her failure to challenge a popular president, or jeopardise a future presidential bid, had helped lead America into disaster in Iraq.

Many felt they had witnessed a similar triumph of expediency over ideals during her husband's 1992 presidential campaign. On the eve of the New Hampshire primaries, Bill Clinton flew home to Arkansas to preside over the execution of an African-American man named Ricky Ray Rector who had shot and killed a police officer and a civilian during the robbery of a convenience store 11 years before. Rector had also shot himself in the head, and his intelligence was so limited that he saved a slice of pie on the night of his execution – so he could eat it later. Clinton used his support for the death penalty to toughen up his image; after Rector, nobody could accuse him of being soft on crime.

If there was one thing that could be said with assurance about Hillary Clinton as a candidate, it was that she was a woman prepared to work for every vote. Like Bill, she believed in the importance of winning elections. In Iowa, as in her Senate campaigns in New York, she was guided by a few basic rules: start early, raise lots of money, recruit the most experienced staff and build an organisation campaign hard with two or three events a day, and strike back early and forcefully when under attack. The serious groundwork for her presidential campaign began in January 2006 (when Clinton was still denying any plans to run for the White House) with a private dinner for some of the biggest Democratic donors and fundraisers at a home in Georgetown. Clinton then moved to sign up Democratic donors on the west coast.

What was much less clear, compared with the determination of Clinton's campaigning, was what motivated her. Aside from the Iraq war, her votes in the Senate had attracted little attention. She championed no bold ideas, no worthy causes that, while they might prove unpopular in the short-term, were still the right thing to do. On the rare occasions when she did take a strong stand, the issues were unassailable. There were few risks in her vocal support for New York's firefighters after 9/11, for example. Clinton claimed to be unfettered by the ideology of left and right, simply wanting policies that worked. In a 2006 interview with the Washington Post, she pointedly refused to acknowledge an over-arching philosophy, saying: "I approach each issue and problem from a perspective of combining my beliefs and ideals with a search for practical solutions. It doesn't perhaps fit in a pre-existing box, but many of the problems we face as a nation don't either."

The problem was, it was never quite clear what those beliefs and ideals were, and at least some of that confusion seemed deliberate. As Charlotte Mull Young, a high school teacher and committed Democratic supporter in her 50s, noted after an election meeting in the town of Council Bluffs, Iowa: "I think she is a good public servant. I am just not sure who she is serving yet." Clinton's printed campaign material was not that illuminating either. Like all the Democratic candidates, she promised to provide universal healthcare, stop global warming and restore America's standing in the world – but gave few details of how she would do it. Clinton's allies called it pragmatism. It was one of the lessons Clinton carried away from the healthcare debacle of the 1990s: if you think big, you become a target.

Clinton was determined to be an effective senator, and she understood the importance of working with her opponents to get legislation passed. "She didn't want to be just a spear-thrower. She didn't want to be a margin-alised voice that had no impact," said Melanne Verveer, chief of staff when Clinton was first lady. "If there is one way to define Hillary, in my opinion, it is that she is extremely pragmatic. She wants to get things done. She really wants to make progress and she knows that you can't do that in a society like ours unless you bring people together."

But there were additional calculations. If Clinton wanted to win elections, she had to defy categorisation. She had to appeal to an undefined political centre. Since the 1980s, America's two main parties had been losing their influence over voters. Independent voters now made up about 40 per cent of the electorate. A Democratic candidate could no longer take it for granted that a registered Democrat would reliably vote for the party, while the same was true of the Republicans. While Karl Rove, the brains behind George Bush's election in 2000, had devised a successful strategy of firing up the Republican base on issues such as gay marriage to get them to the polls, Clinton (like her husband before her) took the opposite approach. She decided to market herself not to the Democratic base, but to the centre. Did she, in a 2005 speech to a pro-choice rally, soften her support for abortion rights by calling on activists to find common ground with the pro life movement? It wasn't clear, but it was undeniably a play for the middle.

Clinton's campaign strategists believed it was possible to lay concerns about her electability and her core beliefs to rest in Iowa. She could counter her reputation for divisiveness by revealing a warmer, humorous side to her personality, and deflect attention from her initial support for the Iraq war by stressing her promise to end the fighting. They saw the campaign essentially as a rebranding exercise. Although Clinton had been a fixture on America's political stage for years, her strategists believed it was possible to wipe the slate clean. It was a plan that was copied almost entirely from Clinton's run for the Senate, with its listening tours and its focus on smaller venues.

In Iowa that strategy made for a good fit. The number of caucus-goers was small – about 125,000 Democrats voted in the 2004 elections – and it was feasible for Clinton to meet face-to-face with a considerable number of them. She spent several days at a time in the state, turning up at high school auditoriums, pot-luck dinners, and in people's living rooms, to re-acquaint herself with voters one handshake at a time. Some people's ideas about Clinton would remain fixed, however. When she got up to speak at the fairground's main outdoor promenade, a woman yelled out: "Hillary, save our country!" At the back of the crowd, Norman Hjelmeland, a retired nursing home administrator from Des Moines, could barely swallow his disgust. "I have no problem with a woman president, but I do have a problem with *her*. I think she is going to be dictatorial. It's her way or the highway," he said. Carol Ann Kruse, from a rural part of the state, agreed: "When she said she was always for the underdog, that was the biggest joke that there has ever been."

There were limits, too, to Clinton's abilities as a campaigner, and her strategists respected them. On the defining day of her political career – her announcement for the presidency – Clinton addressed the American people on a video posted on her website. It was in itself an admission: the flesh-and-blood Hillary Clinton was no match for the emotional power of a skilfully manufactured video. Although other candidates were harnessing the power of the net, and Barack Obama too made his initial announcement online, they scheduled live events as well. Following her announcement, Hillary Clinton held three webchats.

Unlike Bill, she was not blessed with charisma or instinctive empathy. It was just not her style to reach out to touch or hug a stranger telling a story of personal tragedy. She also lacked the gift of making scripted material seem genuine. When she tried to reprise the theme of her first television advertisement in Iowa – "You are not invisible to me" – at election meetings, she seemed more emotionally distant than the image on screen. And sometimes Clinton simply tried too hard. When she sought to project outrage and indignation, her accent migrated disconcertingly from the Midwest to the American South, and her vocabulary descended a few rungs in social class. Here was a graduate of Yale law school saying "git" and "gonna", and borrowing the metaphors of the late famously flamboyant Texas politician, Ann Richards. "That dog doesn't hunt any more," Clinton told a meeting in Council Bluffs. She meant that the Bush administration's arguments were no longer credible. In the audience, people glanced at one another, and back at the figure in front of them wearing a pinstriped black suit despite the sweltering summer heat. Hunting dogs? This was the Senator from New York, wasn't it? When did Clinton ever hunt?

But Clinton's strategists were basically right. Through tightly controlled exposure, it was possible to repackage a candidate, even one as well known and iconic as Clinton. On the road in Iowa and the other early-voting state of New Hampshire, in school gymnasiums and community halls, Clinton found a campaign style that suited her. The smaller venues did not demand a magnetic personality, or stirring oratory – her husband's forte – but they gave Clinton a showcase for her grasp of policy detail, and allowed her to create an impression of experience. At every event, volunteers handed out brochures with a headline that said: "Ready." Clinton was making inroads.

In the debates, Clinton's answers were crisp and clear, and more often than not, it was she who produced the line that would dominate the 24-hour news cycle. Her style was not emotional, or dramatic, but she was admirably in control of the situation. As Mario Cuomo, the former Democratic governor of New York and himself one of the finest speakers of his generation, saw it: "Bill, the president, is histrionic, theatrical. He's an actor, and he's very good at it. She is a Methodist. She is a Methodist even when she gives a speech. She's orderly. She's logical. She's contained. She's controlled, and she is relentlessly intelligent. She never says anything that is not intelligent. She never says anything that is gratuitous and just fluff. She is cogent and intelligent, and that's an entirely different style. There is no schmaltz."

On the campaign trail, Bill Clinton was rarely in sight, so there were few opportunities to make a direct comparison. Instead, he hovered in the background, raising funds, offering advice, and occasionally taking on his wife's old job of fending off attacks. Hillary made it clear from the outset that Bill would have a limited role in her administration as a goodwill ambassador abroad. As the campaign progressed, it seemed increasingly implausible that he would exert undue influence once his wife was in the White House. Hillary Clinton was in charge, and on the campaign trail she was her own woman.

For all the studied lack of flair, there was no denying the excitement among women that Clinton was a candidate. Unlike an earlier generation of candidates, who struggled to get voters to overlook their gender, Clinton addressed the question head-on. She used her gender as an emblem of inclusiveness, an entree to appeal to poor Americans, African-Americans and Latino voters. She attended the banquet of a national convention of African American beauty salon owners, telling them she understood their culture of hard work and family.

Bill Clinton was nicknamed "America's first black president" because of his empathy for African-Americans, which had made itself felt even while he was a student at Yale. Hillary, who in her own youth had tried to reach across America's racial divide, hoped to benefit from black voters' residual support for her husband. Her strategists believed she could even compete on an equal footing with Barack Obama.

Hillary spoke about education for young people who were not bound for college, and protecting families from loan sharks, and at virtually every campaign stop she drew attention to her gender while apparently doing just the opposite. "I'm proud to be running to be the first woman president, but I'm not running because I'm a woman. I'm running because I think I'm the best qualified and experienced to hit the ground running and get the job done," she said. Clinton was also confident enough to acknowledge a debt to the women's movement. "When I was growing up I did not think that I would run for president," she told a televised debate in Iowa. "But I could not be standing here today without the women's movement."

She made rueful comments about hairstyles – Clinton was ridiculed when First Lady for her multiple image changes – and her unsuccessful attempts to lose weight. She talked not just about her famous husband and daughter, but about her mother, Dorothy Rodham, who lived with her in Washington, DC, and the worries of caring for an ageing parent. She even dared to crack the occasional joke about dealing with her straying husband, telling a crowd she had experience with "evil and bad men".

Women especially viewed such personal disclosures as a sign of sincerity. Some found parallels in their own lives with Clinton's difficulties in her marriage, and saw her as someone who would serve as their champion. "I've loved her from the start, ever since Bill Clinton was president," said Betra Reeves, a single mother of three, and a daycare worker, in Council Bluffs. "Look at all she went through, and they are still together." Others were moved to champion Clinton when it seemed she was being criticised simply for being a woman. When, in an early television debate, John Edwards joked that he did not like Clinton's swirly-patterned quilted jacket, the female population of the blogosphere erupted in indignation. How dare he! Others said they felt instinctively that as a woman Clinton was more compassionate, and better able to understand their lives. And some saw in Clinton, as they did in Obama, a chance to shake things up in Washington.

Among men, the response was decidedly cooler. In July 2007 a poll of Democratic-caucus goers by the University of Iowa found women were much more likely than men to support Clinton as a candidate, and much more likely to consider her a strong candidate. She had the support of 30 per cent of women, but only 18 per cent of men, and while 30 per cent of women thought Clinton was the Democrats' strongest candidate, only 17 per cent of men did. "I think she has good ideas, but I am worried that if she wins the nomination so many people dislike her that in the election we will be handing a win to the Republican candidate," said Marvin Dick, a retired school principal. "Some of it is fallout from her husband's presidency. People who dislike Bill Clinton dislike Hillary Clinton." But deeper forces were at work. "She is a powerful woman, and I think a large number of people have a problem with that."

The morning of the state fair had taken Clinton to Waukee, a small town west of the state capital, Des Moines. Wendy Adato, a paralegal with twin sons, aged eight, had lived in Washington during the Clinton administration, and had thought she knew what Hillary Clinton was like. But she was surprised when she saw her in the flesh. "She seemed a lot more warm – not as stiff as she does on camera. She really seemed to have a good grasp of the issues, and answers to some of the issues," Adato said after listening to her speech. Was Clinton electable? Adato was not sure how voters felt about another Clinton presidency, or that past reputation for divisiveness, but she ventured: "I would say at this point that she is a lot more electable than I thought nine months ago."

Clinton was now presenting herself as a leader of opinion against the war. In a debate in New Hampshire in June 2007, she promised to begin a withdrawal within her first 100 days in office. "If President Bush has not ended the war in Iraq, to bring our troops home – that would be the very first thing that I would do." Six weeks later, in Iowa, Clinton hedged on the dates. She would bring the troops home "as soon as we can". But the shift was overlooked by Ruth Almond, a woman from Council Bluffs. The important thing was that Clinton was now in favour of a withdrawal. "I had a lot of misgivings at first," she said. "If she won me over, I think she can win just about anybody over."

In her website's list of 10 possible reasons to support Clinton for president, number one was to end the war in Iraq. But it had taken five years for Clinton to come full circle on Iraq, from her vote in October 2002 in favour of the use of force against Saddam Hussein to a proposal in May 2007 to repeal Congress's authority for the war. During those five years, more often than not, she trailed other senators in summoning a critique of the war, and of Bush's leadership. The lag seemed to be dictated not by Clinton's reading of events on the ground, or even by ideology – it was an expression of political caution. At every slow shift of public opinion, Clinton was there – or rather one step behind. She was outflanked on more than one occasion by centrist Democrats, and even Republicans. When she did attempt to show leadership on the war – early in 2007 – it was safely from the back, putting forward proposals that were smaller in scope and intention than those under consideration by her colleagues in the Senate. But her position struck a chord with the large number of Americans who had initially supported the invasion. Clinton opposed the war, true, but she was no peace activist. Like them, she had gradually come to realise that the war was a grave mistake.

Her approach was effective in terms of advancing her personal political interests. In the run-up to the 2008 presidential elections, Clinton was widely seen as the strongest leader among the Democratic candidates, defying the notion that a woman was incapable of making the tough decisions required of a commander-in-chief. But that was certainly not the general consensus about Clinton when she was first elected to the Senate in 2000.

She started her career with two distinct disadvantages on defence. She was a woman, and she was married to Bill Clinton, who had avoided going to Vietnam, and been vilified by the right as a draft dodger. She had little time to overcome the presumption that she would be weak on issues of foreign policy and defence. Come 9/11, Clinton had been a senator for less than nine months, and in that time had delivered no major speeches on issues of terrorism or defence. At the time of the attacks, she sat on no committees that dealt with defence or foreign policy, so her Senate staff lacked security clearance to review classified documents. She was also saddled with the record of the Clinton administration on Osama bin Laden and the Taliban.

It was on Bill Clinton's watch, after all, that the fundamentalists took control of Afghanistan. Bin Laden and his followers, meanwhile, had carried out three attacks on American targets: a 1993 car bomb in the parking garage of the World Trade Centre, which killed six people; the simultaneous attacks in 1998 on the US embassies in Kenya and Tanzania which killed more than 220 people; and the bombing in late 2000 of the USS

Cole, which killed 17 American sailors, while the destroyer was on a fuelling stop off Aden. Bill Clinton's attempts to retaliate against Bin Laden for the embassy bombings were an intelligence fiasco. In Sudan, the cruise missile strike destroyed the country's main pharmaceutical plant – not a nerve gas factory for Bin Laden as the CIA had claimed. In Afghanistan, the missiles killed 20 militants belonging to groups fighting the Indian army in Indian-held Kashmir, not followers of Bin Laden. As a senator who was being discussed as a potential presidential contender, Hillary Clinton needed to protect herself from charges that her husband's administration had failed to respond effectively to the threat posed by al-Qaida. She also needed to demonstrate that she had the skills and resolve to defend the homeland. Clinton set out to reinvent herself as America's protector: an advocate of a muscular defence who had an unparalleled grasp of the issues.

On September 12 2001 Clinton issued a statement expressing her support for the White House, and threatening retribution against the attackers, with a line that could have been fed to her directly by George Bush. "You are either with America in our time of need or you are not," she said. Clinton threatened to rain down the anger of the US government on those who were on the wrong side of that divide: "Not only those who harbour terrorists, but those who in any way aid or comfort them whatsoever will now face the wrath of our country." She had forgotten, in the heat of the moment, that as a senator she was in no position to order such retribution.

In the months to come, Clinton absorbed reams of detail about weapons systems, and recruited a retired general, Jack Keane, as an unofficial adviser on military affairs. (Keane would go on to formulate the Bush administration's strategy of pouring more combat troops into Iraq in January 2007.) In 2003 she swapped her seat on the budget committee for one on the armed services committee, gaining a platform and authority to talk about defence. She made her first trip to Iraq and Afghanistan in November of that year, meeting US military commanders on the ground. Clinton was also vocal in her support for the troops. She lobbied for free postage on care packages to troops serving overseas, and championed the needs of combat veterans who had suffered traumatic brain injuries in Iraq. "She became a student of the military. She asked for armed services because she needed to prove herself," said Elizabeth Bagley, the host of that early fundraising dinner for Hillary in 2006. "It was a strategic move." The re-education effort did not go unnoticed; soon senior officials at the Pentagon were praising Clinton's steady judgment on military matters.

On Iraq, however, that judgment failed her, notably on the night of October 10 2002, when she gave a speech in the Senate outlining her decision to support a war against Saddam Hussein. It was, she said, "probably the hardest decision I have ever had to make", but she cast her vote with conviction.

Much has been written about how George W Bush was trying to complete his father's "unfinished business" with Iraq. The first president Bush had gone to war against Iraq in 1991, and encouraged a rebellion that ended in the slaughter of tens of thousands of Iraqi Shias. Two years later, Iraqi agents had been accused of trying to assassinate him in a car bomb in Kuwait. His son talked about that attempt on several occasions. But Hillary Clinton also was guided by a sense of responsibility towards an earlier administration.

She told the Senate during her speech from the floor that her primary concern in casting her vote was freeing the hand of a president who might soon be at war: "My decision is influenced by my eight years of experience on the other end of Pennsylvania Avenue in the White House, watching my husband deal with serious challenges to our nation. I want this president, or any future president, to be in the strongest possible position to lead our country in the United Nations or in war." In explanation, she cited her husband's difficulties in the 1990s in trying to get the support of the UN security council for military interventions in Bosnia and Kosovo — and his battle with Saddam Hussein over weapons inspections.

The statement is striking in its sympathies. A senator for two years, Hillary Clinton identified far more strongly with the challenges faced by Bush than with the duties of an elected official of Congress. She had never been one to challenge the system, not even during her student days at Yale. But her support for Bush transcended her usual deference. Was she guarding her husband's legacy, or was she thinking of her own future in the White House? The Clintons had arrived in Washington hoping that the presidency could be a partnership. When Hillary Clinton decided on that day in the Senate to recount her husband's frustrations in dealing with Saddam Hussein, there was almost a proprietorial interest. She was claiming his administration as her own.

Bill Clinton had used force against Saddam during his presidency. In 1993 he ordered US warplanes to destroy Iraqi intelligence sites. In 1998 US and British jets carried out several days of bombing raids. In October 1998, when he was fighting the threat of impeachment after his affair with Monica Lewinsky came to light, Clinton signed legislation making the removal of Saddam Hussein and regime change in Iraq a stated goal of US foreign policy. The Iraq Liberation Act was the brainchild of a group of neoconservative intellectuals, some of whom, like Donald Rumsfeld and Paul Wolfowitz, would later occupy key posts at the Pentagon during the Bush administration. The act instructed Congress to channel money to Iraqi exile groups to try to overthrow Saddam. The passage of the act was crucial to the Bush administration when it was making its case for war.

In her speech to the Senate, Hillary Clinton accepted without reservation the neoconservative rationale for going to war against Saddam. She betrayed no hint of scepticism about the intelligence – unlike other Democratic senators. Clinton also repeated the Bush administration's charge that Saddam was an ally of Osama bin Laden, accusing the Iraqi leader of giving "aid, comfort and sanctuary to terrorists, including al-Qaida". While she admitted there was no evidence to accuse Iraq of direct involvement in the World Trade Centre attacks, she was not above blurring the lines to suggest that there was, somehow, a connection. "I come to this decision from the perspective of a senator from New York who has seen all too closely the consequences of last year's terrible attacks on our nation," she said. "In balancing the risks of action versus inaction, I think New Yorkers who have gone through the fires of hell may be more attuned to the risk of not acting. I know that I am."

Did Clinton go further in supporting Bush than other Democratic senators? Two of her rivals for the Democratic leadership – Joseph Biden of Delaware and Chris Dodd of Connecticut – voted for the war. But in their speeches both raised concerns about intelligence, and whether Bush was secretly embarked on a project of regime change rather than containing a rogue state apparently developing weapons of mass destruction. "This is not a blank cheque for the use of force against Iraq," Biden told the Senate. Barack Obama, Clinton's strongest opponent, was not elected to the Senate until 2004. In October 2002 he gave a speech to a rally in Chicago denouncing what he called a "dumb war".

Clinton appears to have taken her bearings from the mood of the majority in America that autumn of 2002. Midterm elections were just four weeks away (although Clinton was not up for re-election), and Bush remained a resoundingly popular president. That autumn, the annual survey of global attitudes by the Pew Research Centre for People and the Press found 84 per cent of Americans believed that Saddam Hussein posed a considerable danger to the US. Some 62 per cent were in favour of removing him by force. Clinton was not the only senator tracking the polls. The vote to go to war passed through the Senate 77 to 23.

Clinton has claimed she prepared diligently for the vote. She had kept in close touch with Madeleine Albright, who had served as her husband's secretary of state, and she also called on other members of the Clinton administration for guidance. Her counsellors included Sandy Berger, who had been her husband's national security adviser, as well as Richard Holbrooke, who had served as US ambassador to the UN, and had a reputation as a hawk. Clinton was also among a group of senators who were briefed by the then national security advisor, Condoleezza Rice. She told friends she had sought assurances from Tony Blair that removing Saddam was the right thing to do. There is no record that Clinton sought briefings from foreign policy experts who were critical of the Bush administration's plans to go to war.

Further, as Jeff Gerth and Don Van Natta write in their 2007 biography, *Her Way*, Clinton failed to read the most authoritative assessment by US intelligence agencies of Saddam's weapons capabilities. The National Intelligence Estimate, a 90-page classified report, had been made available 10 days before the vote, and Senator Bob Graham of Florida, the chairman of the intelligence committee, repeatedly urged his fellow Democrats to read it. Only six senators did. It's reasonable to ask why Clinton was not among them, given her usual scrupulous attention to detail. Was she trying to shut out information that could challenge her decision?

The vote to authorise war was not the only piece of Senate business that day. Ten hours earlier, senators were called to vote on an amendment put forward by the Democratic senator from Michigan, Carl Levin, that would restrict Bush's ability to launch a unilateral or pre-emptive strike against Iraq. The amendment would have compelled Bush to return to the United Nations seeking a resolution that specifically authorised the use of force against Iraq, or to seek the approval of Congress. But, as Clinton noted in her speech, she did not believe in setting limits on a president's room for manoeuvre. She voted against the amendment, which was defeated, by 75 votes to 24. Instead, Clinton voted for a diluted amendment put forward by Clinton's mentor in the Senate, the Democratic senator, Robert Byrd, that set a time limit on the use of US forces in Iraq, but allowed Bush to easily override it.

Not long before the first US air raids on Baghdad, a delegation from Code Pink, a women's peace group, descended on Clinton's offices in the Senate's Russell Building to demand a meeting. Nearly 100 women turned up, wearing over-sized pink T-shirts and pink slips over their clothing, and they passed the time by singing until Clinton arrived. The session started pleasantly enough. Clinton told the women they reminded her of pink tulips; the activist Medea Benjamin offered a compliment of her own. "We know that you are a wonderful woman," she said. "Deep down we really think you agree with us."

It took only a few minutes for Clinton to make it apparent that she did not. She offered the same justifications for her vote that she had on the Senate floor five months earlier: the intelligence on Iraq's weapons of mass destruction, her belief that Saddam Hussein would never disarm, and her lack of faith in the UN machinery. The argument did not go down well with the women from Code Pink. The activists accused Clinton of thinking like a man, assuming – falsely – that because she was a woman she had to be on their side. "My impression was that she sounded like George Bush," Benjamin told me four years after that meeting. "Here she was talking to a group of women whom she knew were anti-war and she sounded to us like a man, and like a man who wanted to show that he was as tough and macho as the next guy, and we were really appalled." Benjamin was so outraged by the encounter that she compared Clinton unfavourably with an even more hawkish Democratic senator, Joe Lieberman. Lieberman, at least, had ended his meeting with Code Pink with hugs and tears. "There were others who were more thoughtful about the war and told us what an anguishing decision it was," Benjamin said. She didn't get that sense from Clinton. The meeting between Clinton and Code Pink ended with an activist tossing a pink slip at Clinton in rebuke. Clinton, her jaw clenched, erupted in anger, stabbing a finger at the activists, and saying that as a senator she would never endanger the people of New York. The encounter can be revisited on YouTube.

Benjamin, like many of Clinton's critics on the left, had got it wrong. Clinton was no pacifist. She believed in the use of military power, she believed that Saddam Hussein posed a global threat, and above all, she believed in protecting the powers of the presidency. Although Clinton came of age during Vietnam, and left the Republican party of her upbringing to become a Democrat because of that war, she continued to believe the US military could be a force for good in the world.

In *Living History*, Clinton described in almost lyrical terms a 1996 trip with Chelsea and the musician Sheryl Crow to visit US peacekeeping forces in the Balkans.

"Many voices back home were raising questions about America's role in Bosnia," she wrote. But Clinton was reassured by her chat with the lieutenant who had been deputed to show her around. The young officer had no doubts about the effectiveness of his mission in the Balkans. "Wherever we go, the kids wave at us and smile," he told her. "To me, that's reason enough to be here." Three years before that visit, in 1993, Hillary Clinton had met the writer Elie Wiesel. Wiesel, a survivor of the Holocaust, had pleaded with her to stop the slaughter in the former Yugoslavia. Hillary writes that she was disgusted by the failure of the United Nations to act to stop ethnic cleansing. "I was convinced that the only way to stop the genocide in Bosnia was through selective air strikes against Serbian targets."

Iraq was not the Balkans, but Clinton stood by her decision to go to war long after other Democratic leaders declared that their support for the invasion had been a mistake. In December 2003, a day after Saddam Hussein was dragged out of his hidey-hole, she gave a talk at a New York think tank, upholding the soundness of that vote. "I was one who supported giving President Bush the authority, if necessary, to use force against Saddam Hussein." She had her disagreements with the administration about its failure to build an international coalition on Iraq and its schedule for the handover of sovereignty, but Clinton said she was not pessimistic. Neither was the American public at that point in the war; 59 per cent believed the war had been worth it, according to a Washington Post/ABC News opinion poll.

But as the war in Iraq entered its second year, and it became increasingly obvious that the US invasion had led to catastrophe, Clinton's faith began to look misplaced. By June 2004 a majority of Americans believed the war had been a mistake. "By any reasonable standard our policy in Iraq is failing," Senator Ted Kennedy told reporters towards the end of 2004. A colleague of Clinton's on the armed services committee, he had opposed the war from the outset. In early 2005 the Democratic leader in the Senate, Harry Reid, called on Bush to spell out an exit strategy.

But Clinton remained wilfully blind to the realities of Iraq, and even to the violence that exploded around her during a visit to Baghdad. During her second trip to the city, in February 2005, security conditions were so grim that senators were forced to travel by helicopter between the airport and the Green Zone. But Clinton, who never left the Green Zone, told reporters that parts of Iraq were "functioning well". A few miles outside the American fortress, a half dozen suicide bombers blew themselves up in a crowd of Shia worshippers marking the festival of Ashura, killing more than 50 people. "The fact that you have these suicide bombers now, wreaking such hatred and violence while people pray, is to me, an indication of their failure," Clinton told reporters.

Far from the Green Zone, public opinion on Iraq was shifting. In June 2005, for the first time, a majority of

Americans, 52 per cent, rejected Bush's argument that the war in Iraq was essential to their security, according to another Washington Post/ABC News opinion poll. Nearly 60 per cent said the war was not worth fighting any more, and 40 per cent compared the situation in Iraq to Vietnam.

Other Democratic leaders repudiated their votes to go to war. On November 14 2005 John Edwards wrote in the Washington Post that he was wrong to have supported the war. The following day Jack Murtha, a decorated Marine veteran and a congressman from Pennsylvania, called for a withdrawal of US forces. Although Murtha had voted for the war in 2002, he now believed: "The US cannot accomplish anything further in Iraq militarily." He added: "It is time to bring them home."

Twelve days after Murtha threw down his challenge, Clinton made her move. On November 29 2005 she sent a letter to constituents, accusing Bush of misleading Congress to support the invasion, and warning against an "open-ended commitment without limits or end" in Iraq. "Based on the information that we have today, Congress never would have been asked to give the president authority to use force against Iraq," she wrote. But she refused to offer an apology for her vote, and she opposed setting a date for withdrawal.

Even with those limitations, Clinton was slowly beginning to distance herself from her war vote. But she had no intention of moving ahead of the American heartland, even if that led to criticism from the Democratic base. In

July 2006 she was booed at a meeting of grassroots activists in Washington when she refused to consider imposing a timetable for the withdrawal of US troops, or what she called a "date certain".

By November 2006 anti-war sentiment had swept the Republicans from Congress in midterm elections, and it was clear something had to give. Donald Rumsfeld, the Pentagon chief who had been one of the prime movers for the war, stood down a day after the elections, but it was not enough to stop Republican discontent with the war. In December 2006 Gordon Smith, a Republican senator from Oregon, delivered a broadside against Bush's leadership that was equal parts rage and sorrow. "I, for one, am at the end of my rope when it comes to supporting a policy that has our soldiers patrolling the same streets in the same way, being blown up by the same bombs day after day. That is absurd. It may even be criminal. I cannot support that any more," Smith told the Senate. "Either we clear and hold and build, or let's go home."

By January 2007, 70 per cent of Americans believed the war was going badly. Bush was compelled to offer a change of strategy and ordered 30,000 more troops into combat. Clinton, by now an official candidate for president, made a move of her own. In February 2007, soon after another visit to Iraq, she proposed a cap on existing force levels in Iraq – not a withdrawal. "If I had been president in October of 2002, I would have never asked for authority to divert our attention from Afghanistan to

Iraq, and I certainly would never have started this war," she told the Senate. "But we are where we are." A few months later, Clinton returned to the Senate with a proposal to repeal the original 2002 vote for war. Again there was no apology, but Clinton had recanted. Or had she?

Despite the newly combative rhetoric against Bush, Clinton argued that US interests in the Middle East and the region's security made it essential to keep US troops on the ground. In a March 2007 interview with the New York Times, Clinton admitted she would maintain a significant military presence in Iraq to contain al-Qaida, protect the Kurds, prevent Iran from exercising undue influence, and provide logistical support to the Iraqi government. "I think we have remaining vital national security interests in Iraq," she told the Times. "I think it really does matter whether you have a failed province or a region that serves as a Petri dish for insurgents and al-Qaida." What she did not say was how big a force she would leave behind, or how many bases would be maintained.

Medea Benjamin and other activists were as unforgiving of Clinton's glacial retreat on Iraq as they were of her original vote to go to war. "It's not a change of heart, or a change of thinking, or a principled reflection on the right thing to do," said Benjamin. "It's a purely political move because she recognises that is what the voters who might vote for her want her to do." Some liberal commentators argued that Clinton lost sight of her genuine beliefs because of her desperation to hold the middle ground and build up her military credentials, yet there is a surprising willingness on the left and among feminists to give Clinton a pass on the war. Why undermine the woman who stands the best chance so far of being elected president? As Gloria Steinem told me: "We envisaged all kinds of women running for president, not just one kind of woman. We hoped and prayed for self-respecting women, not someone like Margaret Thatcher. [Clinton] identifies as a human being. She doesn't vote against milk for children like Margaret Thatcher, or oppose the women's movement like Margaret Thatcher."

The shifts in position on Iraq were the most visible result of Clinton's strategy of clinging to the middle ground. But they were not the only instance.

In American politics, there is a term that operatives call the Sister Souljah moment, when a candidate breaks publicly with one of his or her prime constituencies in order to demonstrate they are not a hostage to special interest groups. It's a bit of theatre, not so very different (if a little more dramatic) than Clinton's stroll around the Iowa state fair. The manoeuvre takes its name from an episode involving her husband. During his run for the White House in 1992, Bill Clinton went out of his way to lash out at a hip-hop artist and activist called Sister Souljah, who had made some foolish comments about attacking white people, and he deepened the sting by delivering the rebuke during a speech to African-American activists.

Hillary Clinton's Sister Souljah moment arrived in

January 2005. During a speech to women's organisations to mark the anniversary of the legalisation of abortion in the US through Roe v Wade, Clinton caused outrage by suggesting that supporters of reproductive rights try to find common ground with pro-lifers. "We can all recognise that abortion in many ways represents a sad, even tragic, choice to many, many women," she said. The remarks came as a slap in the face to the reproductive rights movement. Over the years, it had lost a series of legislative battles to the religious right. These defeats had cut off access to abortion for poor women – because there was no federal funding for terminations – and reduced the numbers of clinics in many states. In some parts of the country, like Mississippi or South Dakota, only one functioning clinic remained. In most states, it was illegal to perform an abortion on a minor without first notifying her parents, and it was impossible to find a clinic that would perform an abortion after the first 12 weeks of pregnancy.

Clinton compounded the offence by offering praise to religious organisations that encouraged teenagers to abstain from sex until after they were married. As president, Bush doubled funding for abstinence education, and funnelled much of the increase through evangelical groups. The largesse came at the expense of programmes providing information about contraception or sex education, and at a time when Bush was cutting funds for infant health and after-school programmes. "I respect your values," Clinton told the anti-abortion lobby, and asked conservatives to join her in supporting family planning. "There's an opportunity for people of good faith to find common ground in this debate. We should be able to agree that we want every child born in this country to be born, cherished and loved."

Faye Wattleton, who was president of the Planned Parenthood Federation of America for 16 years before founding the Centre for the Advancement of Women, was taken aback by Clinton's suggestion that there was a moral equivalency between the anti-abortion lobby and the women's rights movement. Her remarks did not quite rise to the level of betrayal, but "this was an attempt to reposition her stand on reproductive rights in a way that would hopefully comfort people who are not in favour of women having reproductive rights," Wattleton said. "Her positing that those of us who believe the law should stand, and that women should be able to make this choice, were as extreme as those who burn clinics and who picket because they feel strongly and deeply emotional about this issue was really surprising and deeply shocking."

The speech was a significant departure from Clinton's past pronouncements as First Lady and her voting record in the Senate. Although she had talked effusively about the importance of her Methodist faith – especially on the campaign trail – Clinton had shown no sympathy for the religious right in her votes. She had been unwavering in her support for abortion rights. She opposed attempts to ban a procedure for terminations performed during the middle months of pregnancy that the right calls partial-birth abortions, and laws that would require minors to get parental consent for an abortion. She voted against the confirmation of two of Bush's judges on the Supreme Court, both of whom were anti-abortion, and she attacked the Bush administration for delaying the release of the morning-after contraceptive for years because of pressure from the religious right. So why would Clinton seemingly spurn the very same causes she espouses – and in such a public way? "Maybe she believes that what she has to do is to be cautious," said Wattleton. "Her adaptation to political expediency is sort of the establishment way of doing things."

Mario Cuomo, who for years dominated the Democratic landscape in New York, has a story he likes to tell that illustrates the Clintons' brand of political campaigning. In 1996, when Bill Clinton was running for a second term as president, the two men had a backstage chat following an election rally. Cuomo's political career was over by then, but he urged Clinton to adopt a cause in the time remaining before voting day, and take a bold stand. In Cuomo's account, Clinton listened respectfully to the former governor. Then he took him by the shoulders, and said sadly: "But you *lost*." Cuomo acknowledges that the Clintons' formula for elections has proven to be a winning one: campaign hard and campaign rich, keep an eye on the middle ground, take no unnecessary risks. As front-runner, Hillary Clinton would be foolish to redraft a message or shake up a campaign machine that is to all appearances working. Why make the road to the White House any more difficult? But Cuomo argues that that strategy, though effective during the campaign, carries a heavy price. On the campaign trail, Clinton was reluctant to spell out her stand on relatively mundane issues, such as whether she would support higher fuel economy standards. She was equally cagey on healthcare – the most important domestic issue in the 2008 race. She did not roll out her plan for healthcare until several months after her main rivals, Obama and Edwards – and then she appeared to have borrowed heavily from them and thrown overboard the ideas that drove her proposals in the 1990s.

Caution has been Clinton's lodestar. By clinging to the political centre, she has insulated herself from attack from the right. But if she becomes president, her timidity will make it difficult to carry the public along if she wants to effect real change. Voters are attracted to her because of her image of experience, or solidity as a candidate. If elected, Clinton will be bound by her promise to end the war in Iraq. But her mandate runs no further. True, Clinton's strategy has put her ahead of her rivals for the 2008 elections. But what about afterwards? As Cuomo said, "What you give up when you win is leverage."

CONCLUSION

The two-president family could soon be an American tradition. If Hillary Clinton is elected, and if she wins a second term, the Bushes and the Clintons between them will have occupied the Oval Office for 28 consecutive years. The Bushes, father and son, are outwardly casual about their shared experience, and it's just about possible to imagine them sitting around the breakfast table comparing notes on the wars they each waged on Iraq, and the fickle nature of the American electorate. They use presidential codenames. George Herbert Walker Bush is "41", his place in the line of presidents that began with George Washington. His son, George Walker Bush, is "43" But what if Hillary Clinton becomes number 44? It is hard to picture her and Bill addressing each other by their presidential numbers.

The Bushes and Clintons also have very different approaches to dynastic rule. George W Bush distanced himself from his father's record; after all, George HW Bush was voted out of office. But in her run for the Senate, and now for the presidency, Hillary Clinton has seen her husband's legacy as a positive.

Bill Clinton had a 65 per cent approval rating when he left the White House after his second term. The benefits to Hillary of that popularity outweighed the risks of being seen as stuck in the past. And so she has appropriated her husband's eight years in the White House as her own, casting her time as First Lady as an apprenticeship to the presidency. She has watched and learned. She knows who to call to get things done; and when she doesn't ... well, there is a former president she would not hesitate to ask for advice.

In an age when security ranks near the top of Americans' concerns, Hillary Clinton's understanding of how the White House works has been one of her greatest assets. She has also run on her performance as a senator and her ability to connect with the people of New York state. In office, she has shown a flair for constituency work, for recruiting capable staff to serve the region that elected her. She understands the linkages between the worlds of academia, government and business, and has sought to use those linkages to help New Yorkers. On the campaign trail, she has radiated competence: quick and fluent in televised debates, unthreatening in the evening webchats she favours over conventional press conferences. When she has come under fire from opponents, like fellow New Yorker Rudy Giuliani, Clinton has hit back.

She has assembled and presided over a sophisticated election machine that has reached out to both centrists and her party's liberal base, and dampened Democratic fears that she was unelectable. As it turns out, Democrats, especially women, do like Clinton, or at least respect her, or are resigned to her. "She's it, so I like her," said a former Democratic senate staffer who now works for a large Washington law firm. It has not gone unnoticed that Clinton has used her influence in the Senate to promote other women, from the team of trusted aides known as Hillaryland to fellow Democrats running for election.

But despite Clinton's achievements in her own right, a debt to her husband's administration has come as part of the package. On key decisions such as the Iraq war, she has relied on her husband's experiences and his team of advisers. Those ties, coupled with Clinton's natural inclination to caution, have limited her capacity to develop new initiatives, or to think in fresh ways about the concerns that have emerged since her husband left the White House. On issues from the war in Iraq to global warming, Clinton has led from behind.

To some extent, the backward cast of Clinton's leadership is a function of her life story. Much like the earlier generation of women who inherited their seats in Congress, Clinton got her start in elected politics because of her spouse. Viewed globally, against the recent history of South Asia, where India, Sri Lanka, Pakistan and Bangladesh have all been led by women who rose to power after the death of husbands or fathers, Clinton's ascendancy seems to be more about the preservation of tradition than change.

Most of Clinton's life – certainly her married life – was a process of accommodation to entrenched power. As a Yale law student at the age of 22, she kept her focus on her studies while the world around her was in a state of upheaval over Vietnam. At 27, she subsumed her professional ambition to her husband's career, turning her back on the contacts she had made while working on the Watergate hearings in Washington in order to join Bill in the backwater of Arkansas. At 35, when Bill's career appeared stalled after he had served a single term as governor, she invested her energy in his comeback. There was no serious conversation about switching focus to her career – at least none that was recorded by biographers. At 41, she sacrificed her pride and personal privacy to discuss her troubled marriage on television and save her husband's campaign for president. It was not until she reached her mid-50s that Clinton began to pursue her own political agenda when she ran for Senate.

Clinton's record in the Senate and on the campaign trail reveals a person who identifies with authority as a matter of instinct, and who shies away from leadership on the big issues. As president, however, she would be that authority, and it remains unclear what her grand vision is

– if indeed she has one. Clinton's focus on incremental change – the lesson she took away from the healthcare debacle of the 1990s – has made her an effective advocate for the people of New York. But what kind of president would she make? At the very least, she would be able and hard-working and surround herself with the best possible professional advisers. That is not intended to seem belittling. After the grand imperial vision of Bush's presidency – and the death and squalor that resulted in Hurricane Katrina and Iraq – a safe pair of hands might be just what America needs.

ACKNOWLEDGMENTS

This book would never have appeared at all if not for Lisa Darnell, whose idea it was, and my colleagues at the Guardian who offered their support. I am grateful to Harriet Sherwood, the Guardian's foreign editor, for giving me the time to work on the book, and to Ewen MacAskill, for collegiality and sound advice. Phil Daoust was the deftest of editors. I am indebted to Paula Newberg for giving my emerging ideas some degree of coherence and shape. The following people helped make the book much better than it otherwise might have been: Richard Adams, Helen Brooks, Monica Contreras, Barbara Davidson, Siddharth Dube, Kathy Gannon, Nicole Gaouette, Ruchira Gupta, Eric Hilaire, Danna Jackson, Angella Johnson, Ron Kampeas, Carol Keefer, Jennifer Lawson, Andrew Metz, Anita Peltonen, Ed Pilkington, Ari Posner, Leslie Rose, Ornit Shani, Shauna Lani Shames, Christine Spolar, Michael Tomasky, Roger Tooth and Melinda Wittstock. I am very thankful. Any mistakes or failings are of course my own. Thank you as well to the folks at Affinity Labs for a congenial work environment. Most of all though I am thankful to my parents, Sheila and Gerald Goldenberg.

INDEX